D0887340

John Donald O'Shea "hits it out of the park" with *Memories of the Great Depression: a Time Remembered*. While his first book was darn good, this one is "5 stars." I felt I was with the characters in this book as they describe their old neighborhoods, eke out their meals, and struggle to survive. I was captivated and transported back nearly 100 years. A "must read."

— Bonnie Keiner
Endorsed Educator: History and English.
Endorsed also by the Wharton School of Business in New Product Introduction; Product Management; Financial Management; and Life Cycle Management

The stories gathered in this book—abundantly recall memories of long-ago days—are less a nostalgic journey, than a reminder both of the toughness and courage of the human spirit, as well as, how people managed to fare without so many of the conveniences and safety networks that we take for granted today.

The depth of their human decency is evident throughout, and they speak of common, shared experiences that are increasingly rare today.

— Gregory D. Cusack — retired college teacher (American history and political science); former member of Iowa House of Representatives and Davenport City Council

The story-tellers paint word-pictures of the lives they knew during America's Great Depression of the 1930s — individual accounts, detailing a common experience. These are stories of how ordinary Americans dealt with daily life during a period when the American economy tanked. It's a history that our children need to know.

— Thomas Longeway — CEO Classic Sunglasses, LLC. Retired

[Judge] O' Shea delivers the story of the Great Depression, and of the sacrifices the American people made in deeply trying times prior to and during the war. It paints a vivid picture of how families managed to endure during a most difficult time in America.

The stories throughout capture the essence of self-reliance, as well as reliance on others. The idea of "we are all in this together" is woven through the fabric. His ability to tell the stories of individuals, kids, workers, the down-and-out, as well as those not as deeply impacted financially by the Depression, is inspiring.

I strongly recommend *Memories of the Great Depression: A Time Remembered* to those of us born and raised just after the Greatest Generation. It is my recommendation that it be made available as an historical reference book for the generations to come.

— Joseph P. Murphy — Vietnam Veteran 1968-69

The storytellers — ordinary Americans — recall the times in their lives when dust storms blotted out the daylight and suffocated breathers; and the depressed economy forced thousands of people into poverty and bankruptcy.

Readers of *Memories of the Great Depression: A Time Remembered* will learn the history of America's "Great Depression of the 1930s" at the grassroots level.

— Frank Lyons — engineer and writer

Memories of the Great Depression

A TIME REMEMBERED

John Donald O'Shea

CrossLink Publishing
RAPID CITY, SD

O'Shea/CrossLink Publishing
1601 Mt Rushmore Rd. Ste 3288
Rapid City, SD 57701
www.CrossLinkPublishing.com

Ordering Information:
Quantity sales. Special discounts are available on quantity purchases by corporations, associations, and others. For details, contact the "Special Sales Department" at the address above.

Memories of the Great Depression: A Time Remembered/John Donald O'Shea.
 —1st ed.
ISBN 978-1-63357-260-7

Library of Congress Control Number: 2020943178

Contents

Preface

Why have I written this book? The answer is simple. In writing my first book, *Memories of the Great Depression: A Time Forgotten*, the process of gathering first-hand personal accounts of people who lived through the Great Depression of the 1930s and preserving them became a labor of love.

My great regret is that I came late to the task. By the time I did, my mother and father were dead, as well as almost all of their siblings and friends. Their memories went with them to their graves. As I sit at my computer this January 19, 2022, fewer and fewer persons remain who lived through and survived the Great Depression.

Most historians tell us that the Great Depression began in 1929 and ran into the World War II years. Some argue that it continued until the end of the war. Therefore, to have a memory of the twelve years from 1929 through 1941, a person would have had to have been born early in 1926. That would make them about ninety-five years old today.

The people who grew up during the Great Depression are the same people who soon selflessly exchanged their civilian clothes for military and naval uniforms. They fought the war—and many of them died—to preserve a free America and the Western tradition of democracy. In the 1941 words of FDR, we fought so people in the free world could continue to enjoy the "Four Freedoms"—freedom of speech and worship; freedom from want and fear. It was this generation of Americans, raised during the Great Depression, who freely faced death and disability in the war, who have most appropriately been labeled "Our Greatest Generation."

The period from 1929 to 1941 was truly a "transitional" period. On the farms, cars, trucks, and tractors were slowly replacing horses. In the cities, the transition was swifter. But as late as the 1940s in Chicago, I can still recall horses plying the alleys, pulling the wagons of the "Rags, old iron men." And I can recall my grandfather's bottling company's chain-driven delivery trucks, which were still in use in the early 1950s.

For the people on the farms, and even in the small towns, during the 1930s, modernization came more slowly. Central heating had not yet taken the place of the wood cook stove in the kitchen, or of the kerosene stove in the dining room. Electrification of the farms was years behind that in the big cities. Many farm radios operated on batteries. Kerosene lamps were the norm. Few farmhouses had running water or indoor toilets. The outhouse was still in common usage, and with it, the Sears catalog.

The 1930s were a time when people made do with what they had. For most Americans, it was an era of hand-me-downs, darning socks, and making do with the bare necessities.

For the more well-to-do, of course, there were still luxuries. But the wealthy who had common sense took care not to flaunt their wealth, while the wealthy with compassion used significant portions of their wealth for civic improvements and to help the poor and destitute.

Today, the idea of waking your deceased father in the living room of the family home would be unthinkable. But in the 1930s, when families had little or no money to spare, the dead were waked in their own parlors. A new baby sister, born just before Christmas, was considered the family's Christmas present! Watching a goldfish swim in his bowl sitting atop the console radio was the "early television" of the 1930s.

And it was an age when faith in God animated many lives. Neighbors shared with neighbors. When a father died, his neighbors would provide little jobs for their deceased neighbor's sons. Neighbors and families would hand down used clothing. Firemen would refurbish broken toys to create Christmas presents for children who would otherwise go without. The wealthy built WMCAs, YWCAs, and large dormitory facilities for those without shelter and for young, single women who came to the cities looking for work. Food was routinely provided for "hobos" who came to the door in search of a meal.

It was an era when a girl could find her vocation as a nun either in the kindness and vibrance of a nun teaching at her school, or in a Gene Autry movie—in which Gene returned to find that the girl he loved had taken the nun's veil. It was an era where a father could stand in his yard and point to the sky and show his daughter where God was. It was also an era during which the deacons of the old Baptist church would sit in their reserved places in the front of the church, proudly wearing their best black Sunday suits and spats about their ankles—and when, at the prescribed time during the service, they would lift up the floorboards behind the pulpit to expose the baptismal water into which the minister would then plunge the baptismal candidates.

It was a time when children, and even adults, knew they were poor, but knew everybody else was, too. (You knew you were poor when you had to wear an itchy old woolen swim suit.)

But looking back now, most of the young people who grew up during the Depression would say,

> "Being poor didn't hurt us. The Depression taught us all a lot of lessons. It made us stronger. In some ways it was a very simple time, because nobody had a lot. What made it bearable was that if you went without, you knew your friends also were going without—as long as you had food."

But if life seemed normal to the children raised during the Depression years so long as they had food, things were not normal for their parents and other adults. It was not uncommon for a parent to scavenge the city dump for food to feed his family, or to cut dandelions along a railroad track to harvest greens for dinner. Adults remembered and they saved. They feared the coming of the next Great Depression.

> "I think people who were a little older were affected more by the Depression. I had older cousins and friends that I remained in contact with throughout my

life. They never got over the need to have things— to have possessions. I've always felt I had enough. I've always felt very fortunate to have had 'enough.' I never felt deprived."

The accounts contained in this book are the original, first-hand stories of folks who lived through the Great Depression. I have taken their accounts as they were given to me on my tape recorder. I have changed nothing of substance, but I have organized the materials to create coherent accounts and to avoid redundancies. And of course, I have supplied the punctuation. But the stories are entirely theirs; not mine.

John Donald O'Shea

Note: If you have a story of life during the Great Depression that you would allow me to use in a possible sequel to this sequel, please contact me at irishplaywright@gmail.com.

CHAPTER 1

WHEN I WAS A BOY, MY DAD HAD TWO REMEDIES WHEN WE GOT SICK. THE FIRST CONSISTED OF A BAG OF STEWED ONION SPREAD ACROSS THE 'PATIENT'S' CHEST. THE SECOND WAS A SPOONFUL OF KEROSENE SWEETENED WITH SUGAR.

- WILLIAM "WILLIE" MCADAM -
(Born 1928)

"Hey, don't throw that out!"

"But Daddy, it's no good; the expiration date has passed."

"I'm a Depression baby. We never heard of expiration dates. We tasted it or smelled it. If it wasn't sour or stinky, we kept it."

My kids have heard me say that many times about the "old days." And they have had no desire to hear again "how we flattened both ends of tin cans and squeezed toothpaste tubes completely flat during the war." So, they would quietly leave the stuff by the garbage can and let the old man takeover. I could hear the faint mumbling, "I wish he would get off that Depression stuff."

My father was William McAdams. My mother was Helen Davis. Both of my parents were born in Missouri. Dad was born in 1893, and Ma in 1904.

My parents, William and Helen Davis McAdams, had three children. I was born in 1928. My brother David was born in 1930. And my sister, Helen McAdams Allen, was born in 1931. I was named after our dad, and my sister, Helen, was named after our mother.

My mother's father was Charles Davis. His father was Leslie Davis. Leslie Davis was born a slave in 1852 in Missouri. He last saw his mother at a slave auction when he was nine years old. Great-grandfather Leslie died a free man in Illinois in the 1920s. My mother talked about how much she cared about him. She wondered if anyone else remembered him.

Grandpa Charles Davis had always been a farmhand until he received a letter from a friend who had moved to Moline. That friend told Grandpa that he was making $15.00 a week! That was double the $7.50 they had been making on the farm. Grandpa decided to see for himself. He told Grandma Georgia, his wife, that he was going to Moline to look for a better-paying job. Before long, Grandpa began sending Georgia cash in an envelope to pay their bills. One day, he put in extra cash. Grandma Georgia immediately announced to their two children, Helen (my mother) and Chester, that, "We are going to Moline!"

In 1912, my Grandmother Georgia, with Helen, age eight, and Chester, age five, arrived at Moline. Later, Grandpa and Grandma had two more children, Martha and Chuck.

When Grandma Georgia, Helen, and Chester arrived in Moline, the family moved in with Grandpa's sister, Matt, who was married to Will Bishop. The Bishops lived in the front unit of a small duplex at 1616 9th Street, Moline, with their three children, Della Mae, Pansy, and Leon. Years later, my mother, Helen, told me, "Lord, I don't know how we all lived there! But that's the way folks did it in those days."

After a while, Grandpa Charles and Will Bishop found better-paying jobs in canal and road construction. They then moved their families farther east to the 27th Street and 10th Avenue neighborhood of Moline. Eventually, Grandpa Charles found employment at John Deere.

While Grandpa Charles Davis was working in one of the John Deere plants, he became acquainted with a number of men who had served in World War I. One was a fellow Missourian named William McAdams. Like Grandpa, William McAdams was a very religious man. But unlike Grandpa, he loved to dance. Their friendship soon expanded to include the whole Davis family (including Aunt Matt and Uncle Will Bishop).

My father had come to the Quad Cities with a few friends and cousins, and lived at first in East Moline. Eventually he moved to Moline. Later, when I took Ma somewhere, she would point at a house and say, "That's where your dad once lived."

Grandpa had previously lost his first wife. Now Georgia died, as did her son, Chester. That left Grandpa's oldest daughter, Helen (my mother), who was in high school, to care for her baby brother Chuck and infant sister Martha. Helen raised her younger siblings with help from her cousins, Della Mae and Pansy. This was just one reason why our families were always very close. That's what families did in those days.

Grandpa and his three children, Helen, Martha, and Chuck lived in the house at 15th Street and 26th Avenue, at the northwest corner of the intersection. It sat directly north and across the avenue from the Tabernacle Baptist Church. Grandpa's house faced south, toward the church. It looked very much like something out of a Grant Woods painting—the one with the older couple standing in front of an old Gothic house. Grandpa remained in this house, with his two teenage children Martha and Chuck, until my dad died in 1935.

Even before my mother met my dad, Ma had a very active social life. She was a very talented pianist. The church members had a hard time trying to persuade "Mr. Davis" (Grandpa) to pay for her lessons. Grandpa finally gave in and fifty years later she was still playing for the Tabernacle Baptist Church. Later, she would take her two siblings with her to Chicago, and all three lived with another one of Grandpa's sisters while Ma took training for a job back in Moline.

When William McAdams (my father) met my mother, she was a recent Moline High School graduate. By that time, she was the regular pianist for the Tabernacle Baptist Church. Ma said that Dad was very patient with her while she decided just how serious their relationship was going to become. When their courtship turned serious, it was soon followed by their marriage. In August 1926, they became man and wife.

The newlyweds, William and Helen McAdams, rented a house on the southeast corner of the intersection at 15th Street and 26th Avenue, across the street and directly east from the Tabernacle Baptist Church. The owners were colored. They had originally come from Missouri, as had many in the neighborhood.

Three corners of the intersection of 15th Street and 26th Avenue were then occupied by colored families, with the church on the fourth (southwest) corner.

Our house was a two-story wood frame building. Even then, our house had running water and electricity. A potbelly stove in the living room provided some heat in the house. It and the kitchen stove burned coal. There were grates in the living room ceiling to allow the heat to rise to warm the upstairs. We did not have a hot water heater. Water was heated on the kitchen stove in large pots. We washed ourselves in a wash basin in the sink, or bathed in a large a tub set out on the floor. To do the laundry, water was heated on the kitchen stove and poured into the tub—the same tub in which we bathed. The clothes were then scrubbed on a washboard with Fels Naptha soap chips. They were then hung up to dry on a clothesline. To press the clothes, mother used an iron that she put atop the stove until it got hot.

Our basement had a dirt floor. The walls were slabs of rock. There were shelves along the wall that held many Mason jars filled with preserves that Ma made. There were no inside stairs going down to the basement; the entrance was outside. It was covered by what they called a "grade door."

One day "someone" chopped into that door with a hatchet. David told me about it, and I asked David if Dad looked mad. I told him, "Don't say anything about it." Neither of us was punished, but I would guess that Ma told him he should not have left that hatchet out where his little boys might find it and play with it.

Behind our house, we had a garden, and to the south there were several trees. A boxelder tree in front, near the sidewalk, was my favorite tree to climb because of its long horizontal limbs. There was a cherry tree in back that was also fun to climb, from which Dad would make cherry wine, which he placed in a big crock jar to let it ferment. The biggest tree was an elm tree, which was in the center of our yard. It, too, had its use. Uncle Chuck, who still lived across the street, strung a rope way up high on one of the limbs. He then tied an old tire on the other end. It made a great swing. Then, there was an old wooden door, lying in the backyard, which covered a well from which the pump had been removed. We were constantly cautioned to stay away from it so we wouldn't fall in the well.

We had a telephone during the Depression. Then the bills got too high, and it was removed. I can remember one day the telephone serviceman came in and just took our phone out. During the Depression years, times were very bad. I often heard that people had been "thrown out in the street." Years later, I came across a letter to Dad from our landlady in Chicago, who thanked him for an overdue payment. I don't remember exactly how much he had paid, but I recall that it wasn't even $10. I later learned why she was so thankful. She, too, she was struggling and needed the funds.

Today our old house is always lavishly decorated for each holiday throughout the year with gigantic inflatable creatures, blow molds, colored lights, flags, or anything else that would be an appropriate holiday decoration. When I lived there as a boy, the only decorations we had were soaped-up windows for Halloween.

The Tabernacle Baptist Church in those days played a very large part in our lives. Our church, like many others (white and black), moved to a better location as its membership grew. Tabernacle Baptist Church originally held its meetings in family homes. Then for a while, services were held in the old library building downtown, north of the railroad tracks, on 15th Street. By 1912 a few more colored families had moved into the Moline area, so the church members bought a little church on 7th Street and 15th Avenue. They then moved it to the corner of 15th Street and 26th Avenue. (A newer church building is on that site now, but it is still Tabernacle Baptist Church.) When you walked into the vestibule of the church, you noticed an old rope hanging from the ceiling. This rope must have been connected to the bell in the steeple, but I never heard nor saw the bell.

Because of my restlessness in church (the grownups called it "cuttin' up") when I was very young, I had to sit with the deacons. Grandpa was one of the deacons. For whatever reason, their shoes were laced above their ankles, and they wore a funny piece of cloth with buttons wrapped around each shoe. I think they were called "spats." They were old, stern, serious men. Grandpa had a rule that there was no cooking or laundry done in either of our homes on Sunday. That being said, I occasionally did detect an aroma that certainly was not aftershave. And I know the odor was not coming from my grandfather. It was a persistent rumor that some of the deacons were known to frequent a place called "Old Settlers" in downtown Moline.

I can recall one particular Sunday when all the deacons remained seated. Then, as the congregation began singing, men began lifting up the floor boards behind the pulpit. Next, the Reverend Fulton, wearing a black robe and hip boots, marched up the aisle while reciting scriptures. It suddenly dawned on me that I was about to witness my first Baptism. I was five or six at the time.

The Reverend Fulton then stepped up behind the altar and greeted the candidate, who was also dressed in a bathrobe. Both stepped into the water tank. The Reverend placed his arm under the candidate's back, pinched his nostrils, and immersed him in the water. Then, as they both emerged from the tank, dripping water, I recall the congregation singing "Wade in the Water, Children."

And another similar memory comes to mind. About ten years later, my brother David, my sister Helen, and I were all baptized. By then, I was a pretty big guy, and when Reverend Allen plunged me into the water, my size and weight nearly pulled him under too! (Later, my sister Helen's married name was also Allen; they were not related.)

The Depression affected everybody. Important questions that affected our community were discussed at church. One such question, which was discussed as a matter of church business, was, "What should a boy do when he turns sixteen?"

Should he quit school and help out at home? Should he continue in school and graduate at eighteen? Some boys wanted to quit and help out, but quitting usually meant working at a hotel as a bellhop or in a shoe-shine parlor. Or it could mean joining the CCC (Civilian Conservation Corps) and getting a regular paycheck. Others felt the best choice was to stay in school. My Uncle Chuck made his choice and was very fortunate. He stayed in school and graduated, and then got a job at John Deere. He retired forty years later as a superintendent. For many other boys, the coming of WWII settled the issue.

Ours was a racially mixed neighborhood. The area was called Stewartville.

The first two houses across the street, north from us, were colored-owned—they were owned by the Laniers and Barnes. The rest of the houses on that side of the street were white-owned, including the Bethel Baptist Chapel.

But we were lucky. There just happened to be a large house on 30th Avenue for sale. My folks scraped up enough money to rent and later buy it. Once again, the family lived together in one house. My Uncle Chuck stayed with us, even after he married. He and his wife and their two children stayed with us until after the war ended.

This house was much larger. It even had inside stairs to the basement! And there was even a furnace in the basement! The whole house was heated by hot air through the floor registers. There was running water. But we were not connected to the city sewers; our sewage system drained outside to a septic tank. Periodically, my brother David and I had to clean out the tile pipes which would get clogged up with grease. There was a horrible smell! Ma would have to hire someone from time to time to empty that tank when it filled up. Another set of pipes channeled the overflow toward the low ground between us and 15th Street.

We had a radio. For good reception a wire was connected to it that led to a metal rod outside. That was the antenna. We still burned coal in the kitchen stove and kept food in an icebox on the back porch.

There was a garage, which soon was converted into a chicken house. We raised chickens and always had meat and fresh eggs. On Saturdays, Ma would grab a chicken by its legs and wring its neck. I thought that was too cruel, so I used a hatchet.

There were three empty lots close by. We used them for a "victory garden" during the war. It was normal then to plant a garden. We would plant beets, carrots, asparagus, tomatoes, and potatoes. We also had pole snap beans and peas. There was a grapevine which produced preserves, juice, and pies. We also grew mustard, turnip greens, collard greens, and onions. And rhubarb! We were never hungry—just poor.

There were woods nearby and Uncle Chuck hunted. He provided many rabbits and squirrels, which we ate.

As I mentioned above, the Tabernacle Baptist Church sat at the southwest corner of 26th Avenue and 15th Street. Kitty-corner from the church sat an empty lot, which was shared as a parking lot by the church and Garfield School.

Behind Grandpa's house, on the north side, the land sloped downward to a flat bottom. Actually, it was more like a hollow. That part of the lot was below street and sidewalk level. Grandpa farmed in the hollow. That's where he had his garden. He was a farmer. He planted potatoes and corn down there. From the west side, it was easy to go down there with a mule or a horse. I followed him several times while he plowed. I was only five or six at the time. He also converted an old shack on the property into a chicken house.

Grandpa's house now is long gone. The land behind his house where he farmed has now been filled in. The power company's substation now sits where his house did.

A half-block south from where we lived were a few empty lots and a farmhouse with hogs. My friend Teddy and I wrestled there, and I stepped on a pitch fork. The word "lockjaw" was mentioned, but my folks couldn't afford a doctor. So, band-aids and iodine were applied, and I healed just fine.

A little farther south, 15th Street ended at a deep hollow, which drained under 30th Avenue into a creek. Beyond 30th Avenue was pasture. In those days, 30th Avenue and the southernmost block of 15th Street were not paved. They wouldn't be for years after.

I don't remember too much about my early life. But while we were still in our first house, we three children were taught to say our prayers each night before bedtime. Ma or Dad would be right beside us, and we would kneel down by the bed, put our elbows on the covers, and clasp our hands as we repeated after them, "Now I lay me down to sleep, I pray the Lord my soul to keep." My wife Charlotte and I did the same with our kids. I described this nightly scene to a couple of them many years later and we all laughed because we remembered how one of them fell asleep in that position—knees on the floor and elbows on the bed.

And I can still recall vividly a time when my sister, Helen, was lying in her little baby crib, breathing rapidly and forcefully fighting for her life. She had pneumonia. It was awfully bad. She was just breathing so hard. I could feel the tension and anxiety in the house as we all looked and listened. Everybody thought she was going to die. I didn't understand. I had never seen death before. I didn't know what was going on. But somehow, she survived. She turned out to be pretty tough. I think this was the first time in my life that I became aware of things surrounding me. I can remember hearing them say that she had "bronchitis."

I think one of my earliest memories comes from something that happened when I was out in our backyard playing. I was very young. I heard this loud noise, and when I looked up in the sky to see what it was, I saw this huge cigar-shaped thing. I ran back to hide in the house. My mother or my Uncle Chuck explained to me that what I had seen was a dirigible. That dirigible nearly frightened me to death.

Bicycles were nothing new during this time, but when the balloon tires (pneumatic) were being advertised as a must-have, a boy simply had to have them. Uncle Chuck was working in a hamburger-chili place on 16th Street which has since gone through many changes over the years. It is now a Mexican restaurant. Back in the 1930s it was owned by a black fellow from Michigan. Chuck soon made enough money to buy a Liberty Bike, with fancy tires and fenders. (I may be confusing this bike with a Schwinn model.) I snuck a ride on it once. I fell. Chuck noticed the dent, and believe me, I never touched his things again. Later, it was stolen and never found. But soon afterwards, Chuck's attention turned to Ford automobiles. "Oh, see your Ford dealer, the price is low, and baby how those used cars go! The word is getting all around. Ford used cars are the best in town." Chuck became a believer and for the rest of his life, it was a Ford . . . or a Buick.

When I was a boy, my dad had two remedies when we got sick. The first consisted of a bag of stewed onion spread across the "patient's" chest. The second was a spoonful of kerosene sweetened with sugar. I don't know where he came up with these remedies, but I can remember my mother telling me that Dad was taught to smoke and chew tobacco as a child by his grandmother, who smoked a pipe! So, perhaps . . .

In September 1933, my mother registered me at Garfield School. A short time later, she told me that I had to wait until January to start school because of my birth date. That was the rule in Moline schools. If I had been born in September instead of October 1928, I would have been eligible to start school in the fall. I bawled like a baby. I couldn't understand why.

Two months later, on Monday, the eleventh of March, I left to go to Garfield School. I was six at the time. I had just gotten into first grade. My sister was just three. I had assumed my dad had gone to work. But on the way to school, which was only a half block from our home, I saw him coming down the street with his lunch bucket. That was odd, because he should have been working the first shift then. When I got back home, my mother told me that he came back home sick and had gone up to bed. His bedroom was upstairs. And he never got out of bed again, except to go to the bathroom. I can remember seeing him wearing an old nightgown. I guess a lot of people wore them in those days.

As a little kid, I didn't understand what was going on. David was just going into kindergarten.

But even at my age, I knew that there was a lot of fear and tension among the grownups. They kept using the word "pneumonia." I overheard someone say that "Mr. Mac was getting along better." So, the next day after school, I went out to play with my friend Teddy. Around suppertime, Mrs. Moss came across the street to tell me that I had to come home. My first thought was about my dad. I asked her if he was dead. She answered so softly that I didn't pursue the subject.

Mrs. Moss and I entered the back of the house through the kitchen. A bunch of relatives, mainly those on Ma's side, were already in the living room. I saw some of my cousins for the first time. I remember one named Velma, which was an unusual name to me. We all waited in the living room. Soon two undertakers brought down a wicker basket, carrying my dad's body. The undertakers carried him out of the house and over, I think, to Mr. Brown's Funeral Home in Rock Island. That was Thursday, March 14, 1934.

The next day in school, one of my oldest and best buddies, Frank (Cork) Mahar, was the only one that I can recall who mentioned my dad's death and who offered condolence. How quickly the news of Dad's death travelled in our very friendly neighborhood!

On Saturday, his body was brought back to our house. That's where the visitation was held. We kids were in the kitchen, and every once in a while, we would look into the other room, where my dad's body was, and say, "Oh, he moved!" We still didn't understand what death was—all we could see was that Dad was sleeping. That Sunday, the funeral was held across the street at the Tabernacle Baptist Church. From there his body was taken to the Arsenal Cemetery. One of the members of the honor guard was Mr. Thor, who was our neighbor and the custodian at Garfield School. I remember that some of the gravestones near Dad's grave had the letters "UK" and "COL." Those letters were used by the army to indicate "Unknown" or "Colored." I had no idea what those letters meant. I was only six and a half.

When the family returned home, I remember that Ma checked Dad's lunch bucket. She found an orange and a Milky Way candy bar, which she had cut into three pieces—kind of a symbol for Dad's three kids. It had been in there since Monday morning.

They said he died of bronchitis.

At this time, I was too young to realize the burden of death that had once again settled on Ma's shoulders—three kids, a house, and a very small income. Of course, Grandpa, Chuck, and Martha helped, but I still recall overhearing words like "put out in the street," "bills," "rent," and "overdue."

We three kids didn't see Ma all day, because she worked in other folks' kitchens. When she would return from working all day, she knew how to relax. All those piano lessons she had taken came to good use. Ma would sit down in front of the piano, which had been her wedding present. The three of us kids would watch and listen as she played classical music. And I can remember us saying, "Now here comes the good part"—those runs in Chopin's, Liszt's, and Rachmaninoff's works. We were thrilled! Martha would often join her, and they played duets out of those Modern Music and Musicians Philharmonic volumes, which had also been a wedding present. I still have them in my house, but I still can't play them to this day, because I hated to practice. On the other hand, David loved to sing. Ma accompanied him on the piano, which steered him into becoming a vocalist all his life. I personally believe he still has one of the finest voices I have ever heard. I can still recall him, in later years, playing the role of Joe and singing "Old Man River" in the Quad City Music Guild's production of *Showboat*.

Before Dad became sick, he and Ma were taking evening courses. Dad had earlier taken courses during President Wilson's Administration, and Ma had taken a typing and shorthand course while in high school—despite some teachers trying to discourage her. But after Dad passed away, only domestic jobs were open for her.

Two months after Dad died, on Decoration Day, Ma took me over to the Arsenal Cemetery to visit his grave. We caught the streetcar, got off downtown and then walked to the island. It was the first of many trips over there. The most unforgettable memory that I had was noticing Ma crying at Dad's grave. Sixty-eight years later, I was standing at that same place, and watched the workers open Dad's grave so they could place Ma's coffin in with his.

At the time of his death, my dad was at "Union Malleable," which was part of John Deere. I believe he was a molder. My uncle and my grandfather were both molders.

After my father's death, to pay the bills, my mother did domestic work in other people's homes, right up until the end of the war. Ma seriously considered selling her wedding ring to someone who was collecting gold. To help make ends meet, we had roomers from time to time. To help us, people bought Mom's homemade bread. Mom did most of her cooking from scratch.

I will never forget the kindhearted neighbors who gave us water when ours was shut off. They offered David and me odd jobs, such as cutting their grass, digging their small gardens, window washing, etc.

Some of my clothes came from donations collected by our church. I was always embarrassed when I had to wear knickers — "Little Lord Fauntleroy" outfits. Everyone knew it meant that I was poor. I even had to wear an old, itchy woolen swimsuit when we waded in the Browning Field pool.

David and I would carry home a gallon of skim milk from Anderson's dairy, which was at about 18th Street and 21st Avenue. It was a long walk, and that pail was very heavy.

Ma made root beer. She also made homemade ice cream. Not even candy tasted as good as when we got to lick the dasher.

And I have quite a few memories of my days at Garfield School. Some good, and some not so good. The principal was Ms. Alice Wheelock, from an old, prominent family in Moline. She was considered to be an old maid. Full-time teachers, in order to keep their jobs, were not allowed to get married.

I remember one day I got a called into the office of Mrs. Cross. She said, "I have been watching you all day." I was a little bigger than some of the other boys—and I am sure being colored made a difference. But anyway, she talked to me as if I had been bullying the other kids. I wasn't, but that was a warning to me—"I am always watching you."

But she never seemed to notice the boys who teased and taunted me daily. One time, Joe Daebelliehn spoke out and said, "My mother said they are just as good as we are." Yet, if I got too rough with a kid, she did notice that! I would get called into her office. My buddy Teddy Reid, who was quite familiar with office summons, advised me to "shed tears or cry a little" (fake it, in other words).

Although I was often the object of derision from some of the white boys, I also noticed that they picked on Jewish kids. Jack Zukerman never seemed to let it bother him. He would usually smile and walk away. Even the girls didn't escape this unwanted attention. It has been over eighty years, and I still recall that when one girl would walk by the boys, some of them would hold their noses, lie down on the ground, and pretend that they couldn't breathe because she smelled so bad.

One of the teachers during this time was Ms. Gryce, who told us about the Titanic, and how fortunate her aunt had been to have missed the boat. Until then, I had never heard of that ship, but since then, I have never forgotten the Titanic tragedy.

One of my teachers at Garfield was Miss Warner. Our home was only two or three houses south of where she once lived. She taught our class songs from the slavery days, like "Shortnin' Bread" and she read us stories like "Little Black Sambo." It was commonly understood in those days that, if you were a Negro, your ancestors would have most likely been slaves. I have often wondered if she would have taught us that song and read us that story if she had thought a bit more carefully. Or if she had known, as I have previously mentioned, that my great grandfather, Leslie Davis, who had been born in 1852, had been a slave, and had seen his mother auctioned off at a slave market in 1861. But that's just the way things were in those days. I have never borne ill will toward her. I never felt she meant to hurt anybody.

I also have fond memories of some of the other teachers and staff. It was a great honor when Thor, the janitor, chose one of the boys to ring the bell for everybody to come into the school. He was never "Mister," just "Thor." But when an adventurous kid stuck his tongue on the iron railings (naturally it froze), Thor would come to the rescue. Everyone respected him.

I was in one play about Christopher Columbus. I was a sailor, and my one line was "Look, I see a light!" But Columbus gets all the credit for discovering America in 1492. (The lookout—me!—also helped to discover America in 1492, according to my one line in that school play.)

Whenever I watch a football game and see the players pile up on the ball carrier, I think of a similar grade school game: "Let's play n—r pile." Most of the boys, except for me, would run and jump on an ever-increasing pile of kids and make-believe that they were having fun.

I enjoyed sports but I never had the advantages that many other fellows had. There was no YMCA for me. Until I went to junior high, what I learned, I learned from my buddy, Cork. While at Garfield School, we played a game called "tag ball." A boy named Bob Harrah threw a tennis ball at me, and I just stood there . . . and watched it hit me in the eye. No damage was done, but it taught me that I had a lot to learn about sports.

In the fall, while we were still in Garfield School, Cork would organize the guys into a football team. We'd challenge other grade schools. We'd play wherever we could find an empty lot. Of course, it had to be within walking distance. Our usual football field was at the corner of 15th Street and 28th Avenue, about three blocks south of our school.

That fall, our plans were about to be changed. Someone had driven stakes into the ground to mark off where a new owner was going to build a house. Soon stakes were being knocked over by some of the "gang"—probably with parental guidance—who were unhappy about having a new neighbor. I told my Ma about this, and then I learned that the new owner was a black doctor. He told Ma that he changed his mind about coming here.

He remembered a race riot in Chicago, and seeing his father with a gun in his hand, sitting at a window in their apartment. He didn't want to go through that again, so he left Moline. That lot remained empty for a few more years. Sometimes, when I drive down that street, I look at the house with the brightest, burning red bush at the front door, and I am reminded of the old days when my buddies and I used to play football with no interference from adults.

When I was young, I can remember a "game" that my Uncle Chuck taught me. Chuck was about ten years older than I was. He and his friends were having a party. The game was "postmaster." Chuck taught me to go to one of the girls and say, "I have a letter for . . ." and then I'd name the girl. She'd then come out, and she might get kissed by Chuck or one of his friends.

And then, when I was nine, I can recall getting a newspaper at Carlson's grocery store. The headline said that the German dirigible Hindenburg had crashed and burned at Lakehurst, New Jersey.

And on many hot summer days, we didn't even need a hose. A water department guy would bring out a huge wrench and would open and flush the hydrants, and we would scamper about in the water.

Another thing we did as boys and girls was sit on the curb and watch the cars drive by. In the 1930s, curbs were much higher than they are today, and the streets in Moline were mostly made of paving bricks. There are still some brick streets in Moline; 13th and 14th Streets still have their bricks. In those days, we had a game, the object of which was to be able to identify cars by their makes. On Sundays, the street was full on both sides with parked cars, waiting for the owners and passengers to exit from the two churches. It was fun for us kids to try to identify the different cars. Whoever could identify the most, won. In those days, there were a lot of different makes of cars that are no longer around today—Pierce-Arrows, Duesenbergs, Marmons, Cords, Grahams, Nashes, Hudsons, DeSotos, Studebakers. And of course, there were Pontiacs, and Chevys, Cadillacs and Olds, and Fords and Lincolns . . .

In the evenings, the block was very quiet. I could hear male voices singing the popular songs of the time like "Sweet Adaline," "Darling, I Am Growing Older," "It's a Long, Long Way to Tipperary," etc.

As I grew older, I became very familiar with 15th Street, from the railroad tracks along the Mississippi River all the way south to 30th Avenue. In the downtown area, the library strongly attracted me. I loved to read. And there was a device there called a stereopticon which produced life-like images. The stereopticon was a slide projector that combined two images to create a three-dimensional effect, or make one image dissolve into another.

One time, as I walked back up 15th Street, near 16th Avenue, I noticed a small crowd gathered by the old Roxy Theater. So, I crossed the street to see what was going on. They were all looking at a human-like creature whom they called a "pinhead." The pinhead was staring back at the people who were staring at him. When I squeezed in to get a better look, suddenly the pinhead looked straight at me and laughed. I was highly embarrassed, and needless to say, I couldn't get out of there fast enough. I later learned that a "pinhead" is a person suffering from a condition that results in him having an undersized head.

During the Depression, many men plied the streets to make their living.

In those days, most of us had never seen a refrigerator. The iceman would come down the street. He'd take out his pick and chop off a piece of ice from one of those great big fifty-pound cakes he had in the truck. Sometimes, he'd give us kids who were hanging around the splinters. Nothing tasted so good on a hot summer day! Well, almost nothing. Of course, if we had a nickel or a dime, we could go up 16th Street to Whitey's and get an ice cream cone.

And then there was the ragman. He'd come down our alley and yell something that sounded like, "Oops, allah rags." He was hard to understand, but we all knew he wanted rags.

This was in the days before they had the Goodwill or Disabled Veterans stores. Sometimes, the ragman had a horse-drawn wagon, and sometimes, a truck. When he had a truck, it was fun to watch him stick his crank in the hole in the truck's grill, wind it, and let it go. The engine would cough up smoke, as if it had been sleeping, and the ragman would climb back into his truck.

And milkmen also made deliveries using a horse or a truck. In the wintertime, if the milk was left on the porch too long, it would freeze, expand, and push the cap off. That would expose the rich cream that came to the top to any opportunistic cat who happened to be wandering around the neighborhood. That included our cats!

That was my life in the Depression years and I'm sure millions of folks could tell similar stories.

CHAPTER 2

ON OUR WAY HOME, IT TURNED INTO A BLIZZARD. DAD COULDN'T SEE. SO, HE JUST LET THE HORSES DECIDE WHERE TO GO, AND THEY SOMEHOW GOT US HOME.

- DOROTHY KITTLESON -
(Born May 28, 1921)

My mother was killed in a factory explosion in Des Moines, Iowa. I was three at the time, and my sister was one. Mom had been canning at the time, and she needed lids for the jars she was using. She told me that, "She'd be right back." She went across the street to the store. She had been gone only a couple minutes when suddenly there was a huge explosion. The refrigerator system at the store blew up while she was there and my mother was killed.

After my mother's death, my sister and I went to live with my grandmother at her farm in Worth County. Her farm was on the road that formed the dividing line between Worth and Mitchell Counties. Her home was about a half-mile out of the town of Meltonville, Iowa. The town no longer exists. In those days, it had two grocery stores and an active church.

Grandma's house was a big farmhouse. There was a wood cooking stove. We had to carry the wood in to make it hot. We heated our bathwater on that stove. That's where Grandma canned all our foods.

Besides the kitchen stove, there was also a heating stove. I don't ever recall that we had central heating, but later we had an oil-burning stove in the living room.

After a while, my dad remarried, and he and my stepmom came to live with us at Grandma's. Dad worked the farm there.

When I was young, there were no indoor "facilities" at Grandma's house. We used an outhouse. Later, Dad put in running water.

In the early years there, we had kerosene lamps, which we had to wash every day. The Rural Electrical Cooperative brought in electricity. When we got electricity, it was much nicer.

We never went hungry during the Depression. We had a huge garden. And there were chickens and hogs. In the fall, they always butchered a hog.

During the summers, we would go barefoot all summer long. Our feet were growing fast and shoes were expensive. Then, in the fall, they'd buy shoes for us for school.

In the early years, the road was unimproved. I can recall when they made the improvements. I think that was while I was still in grade school. They graded it using mules.

We had two big horses—Bill and Barney. One winter evening we went to my aunt's house in Otranto, about three-and-a-half miles from our home. We went by horse-drawn sleigh. When we arrived, Dad put the horses and the sleigh in my aunt's barn. While we were there, it started to snow. On our way home, it turned into a blizzard. Dad couldn't see. So, he just let the horses decide where to go, and they somehow got us home.

I began school when I was six, in 1927. Our school was one of five new schools that the county had just built. It was District 5 in Meltonville. It was very modern and nice. It had indoor restrooms, but no running water. But it did have electricity. And we always, as far as I can remember, had a phone.

My younger sister and I were very active in our church. The Episcopalians and the Methodists shared the church. We were Methodists, and we shared our pastor with the church in St. Ansgar.

There were always meetings, and after the meetings, there would be card games and music. The church had an old-style pump organ. I played the piano, but I wasn't able to push the big pedals down to play the organ. So, one of the boys would do that for me.

In the 1930s, there were parties in the town of Otranto. And there were roller skating rinks in Lyle, Minnesota, and in St. Ansgar and Northwood. Once, I fell while roller skating, and I got pretty badly banged-up. There was a nurse there who told me I needed stitches by my mouth. So, we had to find a doctor that night. Getting the stitches wasn't much fun.

There were movie theaters in St. Ansgar and Northwood, but we didn't go to the movies very often. And of course, there was radio.

I had two stepbrothers by my dad's remarriage. My stepbrothers had "horses." They were actually sticks with horse heads. They put them between their legs and pretended they were riding horses. One day, they "rode" down to the grocery store in Meltonville. The grocer, told them that it was too far to walk. My brother told the grocer, "We didn't walk; we rode our horses."

My sister was a year behind me in school. When we graduated, I was seventeen. My grandmother didn't want us to have to take jobs as housekeepers or waitresses, so she insisted that we go to business school. We went to Hamilton Business College. I worked really hard while I was there. When I graduated, they told me that they thought they had something for me. They sent me for an interview at International Harvester, and I was hired, and learned to use a bookkeeping machine. I worked there for two years. Then my sister and I moved to California. The people at International Harvester didn't want me to go.

CHAPTER 3

BY 1931, THINGS HAD HIT BOTTOM. OUR CHRISTMAS GIFT THAT YEAR WAS MY LITTLE SISTER, MARTHA, WHO WAS BORN ON DECEMBER 22, 1931.

- MIKE HOPKINS -
(Born December 11, 1926)

I was born in Colo, Iowa on December 11, 1926. Colo is in Story County, Iowa, about twenty miles due east from Ames. Today, it has a population of about nine hundred people. In the 1930s, its population was only 532. Colo was incorporated in 1876, a century after the signing of the Declaration of Independence.

I was delivered at home in my parents' bedroom. The doctor was our family doctor. I believe his name was Doctor Arthur G. Glann. He had the help of a midwife.

I had two sisters, Veva and Martha. Martha was named after her grandmother, Martha Ray. Veva was named after her mother.

The story of the homes in Colo was a typical story. Farmers would suffer through the years as they worked their farms and saved their money for retirement. Then they would retire to town, and they'd build the house of which they had always dreamed. It would have indoor plumbing, running water, no outside privy, central heat, and electricity. They built what they thought was a monument to their success. For that reason, many of the houses that had been built in Colo were farmers' monuments to success—they had worked hard and saved their money through all those years. They had dreamed about the home they would build—their new place in town.

So, the towns tended to have landmark homes. The earliest houses in town were built in the Victorian style. They would have a turret or a rounded tower that went up two stories.

Our house was a two-story house built in that style. But it had been built in the late nineteenth century by the town's only physician, not by a retired farmer. We had electricity, indoor plumbing. and central hot-water heating. And we had a refrigerator.

The house had a hip roof with a "widow's walk." There was a Victorian railing around the widow's walk on top of the hip roof. This widow's walk was about twelve feet square. A door in the center provided access from the attic. The flat roof of the widow's walk was made of tin sheets that had been soldered together. In high winds, the tin sheets that made up that roof would rattle, and the trap door from the attic would lift up a couple of inches, and then drop back into place. On a dark and stormy night, you had a perfect setting for a Halloween story!

A widow's walk was an architectural feature found in Victorian homes. Widow's walks were common in New England. When a husband went out on the ocean to make his living, his wife could go up to the roof and look farther out on the ocean to see if her husband's ship was coming in. In the Midwest—in Iowa—of course, there weren't any oceans. But it remained a Victorian feature.

In our house, there was a rough stairway in our attic that provided access to the widow's walk. The widow's walk formed the ceiling of the attic. There was no insulation anywhere in the attic; sound could travel from the roof right down through the attic, and right down into the house below. The attic floor was nothing more than a few loose boards spread around to keep you from falling through the second-floor ceiling.

Our house was situated on the last street in town. Our house was in town and taxed as such. Our neighboring farmland was rural and taxed as agricultural.

Our home was situated on an acre of land and had a majestic front yard with four tall pines. The pines would drop their cones all over, and you couldn't mow the lawn until you had picked up the pine cones. Our outbuildings were a chicken house, a smoke house, and a wood shed.

Our home had the typical attached kitchen where you did the cooking on the typical coal-fired or wood-fired cook stove. That part of the house was one-story high. It contained both the kitchen and the pantry. That was also where we would take our milk, and separate it into cream and skimmed milk. The pantry, where we had a kerosene stove, doubled as a summer kitchen. The kerosene stove didn't heat the house up as much as the coal-fired or wood-fired cook stove.

Our dining room was big enough to have the entire threshing crew sit down at the dinner table. There was also a bedroom on the first floor. Then, there was the living room, and there was a parlor. There was a porch across the entire front of the building, with doors that entered into the parlor and into the living room.

Upstairs, there were two bedrooms, a third double bedroom, a bathroom, and a hired man's room.

The early Depression years were good times for wheat farmers. Wheat was thirty cents a bushel. Corn was twenty-seven cents a bushel. Soybeans came later.

The stock market crash, at first, didn't affect the farmers. Early on, prices for wheat and corn remained steady. The "Crash of 1929" changed the picture dramatically for most people. My dad was one of the fortunate few who got his money out of the bank just before the run on the bank.

Our little town of 532 had two banks. One was the McCoy Bank, and the other was the Goodenough Bank. My dad's money was in the McCoy Bank. The owner was my dad's cousin. Coincidentally, Dad just happened to make his withdrawal in time. He had only a small amount deposited there, about $100, but he closed the account and got his money. I was only three at the time, so I didn't know too much.

Then, before long, nobody had any money. Farm commodity prices fell. Hogs brought five dollars per hundredweight at the packinghouse. I can remember my Aunt Mary drawing a bullseye on the barn door, and throwing eggs at it, saying, "That's my target price of eggs!"

We were able to maintain our ownership of our farm during the Depression. Dad had not borrowed much money. Only a very little. The farm was 143 acres. The original farm was one hundred acres, which my parents had bought from an uncle. Later, my mother bought the additional forty acres—a forty-acre field. The farm had not been improved, but it was one hundred percent tillable, with the exception of a couple ponds. One pond was about three acres, and we named it after my mother, whose name was Veva Ray Hopkins. We called it Lake Veva.

We had no money, but we had a big garden. So, we had food. Who needs money! And we weren't alone. Every house had a garden, and every vacant lot was used as a garden.

By 1931, things had hit bottom. Our Christmas gift that year was my little sister, Martha, who was born on December 22, 1931. My older sister, Veva, had been born on July 22, 1925.

At that time, there were still men who worked as farm laborers. They were often paid "in-kind"—perhaps, a side of pork, or a quarter of beef. Casual laborers were paid with milk, eggs, butter, or bacon.

Farmers in those days also worked on neighboring farms. I can recall that we belonged to a "threshing ring." Eight or more farmers would pool their money and buy a threshing machine. A threshing machine or thresher is a piece of farm equipment that threshes grain. It removes the seeds from the stalks and husks. It does so by beating the plant to make the seeds fall out. The machine had a weighing device and a meter, so you paid for each bushel threshed. The money went to the owners of the thresher for their services and to pay for the machine. The owners were called the "corporation." The revenues, minus the expenses, were paid to the members as "dividends." We called the corporation "the Millionaires."

In general, there was an "industrial revolution" in agriculture and farming during the 1920s and 1930s. Little by little, horses were being replaced by monster tractors. At first, these behemoths were steered by a team of horses, hitched to a pole about eight to ten feet long. The horses didn't have to pull, but they provided about two "horsepower" for "power steering."

The early tractors pulled as many as four bottom plows. Out west, they used wheat-disc plows. The early tractors were powered by one- or two-cylinder engines that ran on kerosene for fuel, or they were steam powered. A man driving one of the early tractors had a very difficult time turning the tractor. The early tractors had steering wheels, but in those days, there was no power steering, and it was very, very difficult to turn the tractor just by using the steering wheel and muscle power. That's where the horses came in! They took the same position as if they were pulling a wagon, but they didn't have to pull. All they needed to do was to keep moving in front of the tractor, and steer the tractor by moving the wagon tongue. The tractor moved under its own power, but the horses added the extra steering power that was needed. Without the horses, you really had to muscle the wheel to get the tractor to change its course. The horses provided the power steering!

These early tractors were impractical. They were monsters that required a lot of kerosene. These early tractors were limited to plowing the land or providing stationary power for threshing or sawing firewood. They were good for operating a threshing machine or doing what we called "belt work." They would "belt them up" to a threshing machine or a sawmill. They were a good stationary source of power. Plowing a field with a bottom plow required a lot of care and energy. The early tractors were not practical in the field.

A "bottom plow" is a plow that is designed to go about six inches deep, tear up the turf and completely turn it over. It would flip the turf 180 degrees. A "plow bottom" was the actual part of the plow that went under the sod about six inches. It was being moved forward at about two to three miles an hour, and that was fast enough to cut all the roots that were under the sod. It cut a fourteen- or sixteen-inch swath, or cut. This ribbon of earth was flopped over on its back. When you finished plowing the field, it was all black, which meant that you had turned the soil clear over.

Because the early monster tractors were too big and too clumsy, they were replaced in the late 1920s by real, all-purpose field tractors with steel wheels, and later on, with rubber tires.

Tractors in those days were made by Allis Chalmers, McCormick, John Deere Moline Plow Company, and Twin City Tractor. Twin City tractors were built by the Minneapolis Steel & Machinery Company until 1929. Then it merged with the Moline Implement Company of Illinois and the Minneapolis Threshing Machine Company of Minnesota. The history of farm machinery is an endless story. But in the 1920s and 1930s, the "iron age" of farming was just dawning.

My dad bought a new Twin City tractor. It was a modern, all-purpose tractor. It had been built in Minneapolis. He bought it in 1932, at a time when farm produce prices could still support the payments.

Then we met "Mr. Banker." We kids thought that was his real name! And maybe it was. Mr. Banker would faithfully arrive around noon, once a month. Mother would invite him to stay for dinner. Dad would give him a check, and Mr. Banker would be on his way. Dad was able to make the payments, and we didn't lose the tractor.

The town of Colo had all gravel roads, and the surrounding rural area had farm-to-market roads, which were also gravel. My mother's mother owned land in Maxwell, which was about fourteen miles from Colo. She had a gravel pit on her farm. She sold gravel to the road builders. Her farm was along Indian Creek. My mother's brother, Chester, had drowned on that farm before I was born, in 1921 or 1922. There had been a heavy rain, and the creeks were rising. He went out on horseback to herd the cattle in. He tried to cross through a creek, but the water was going so fast that it swept his horse away. He couldn't get free of the horse and drowned. He was a good horseman, a good rider, and a good swimmer, but he couldn't get free of his horse.

In 1932, Franklin D. Roosevelt was elected President of the United States. At the time of his election, our country was on the edge of revolutionary riots and anarchy. President Roosevelt was a Democrat from a wealthy New York family, but FDR got a lot of his support from conservatives. In those days, the conservatives claimed to be "progressive and liberal." But they didn't know what to do. FDR was a very smart man who could argue in a way that appealed even to conservatives. He also had plenty of money, so he was believable when he said to his conservative Congress, "If we don't do something, this country is going to perish. We have to get the people fed, create job opportunities, and help those who are out of work to gain self-respect again." He used the threat of the country going communist to get conservative support. He told them, "What we've got to do is to get everybody working, put food on the table, and a car in the garage." People during the Great Depression were desperate. They'd say, "If we could only get a job." President Roosevelt's talk about putting everybody back to work and putting food on the table was decried by his opponents as "sloganeering," but his "fireside chats" and government programs gave hope to the people who were out of work. President Roosevelt did it!

At first, "relief programs" were not popular. While I was in school, there were children in school who came to Iowa from Missouri and from other southern states as far away as Georgia. Missouri land was not as productive as Iowa land. So, they'd move up to Iowa, "to where the action was," and where their chances of getting a job would be better. At this time, farmers were leaving their farms, hoping to find jobs off the farm. Some found work on WPA and CCC projects. Roosevelt created many, many relief programs. At first, the word "relief" carried a real stigma. But when unemployed people finally found work, and brought home a paycheck or cash, it was an entirely different story. Then self-respect returned. The Roosevelt administration created farm-to-market roads and instituted the Works Progress Administration (WPA), which built nearly six thousand new schools and other buildings. His programs guaranteed fair prices to the farmers for their crops. This was done by way of setting corn loans at the fair price of corn. If the market for corn dropped below what you owed on your loan, you could surrender your crop. You still had to pay the principle owing on the loan, but the interest would be forgiven.

The Roosevelt administration also created the Civilian Conservation Corps (CCC). The CCC gave young men jobs improving the national parks. The young men would sleep in barracks on cots and be fed regular meals. It was a military-type life, and for some, it was the start of a military career.

When I started school, there was no kindergarten. We started school at age five, and most of the boys would fall in love with their teacher, and the teacher would return their affection. We had a great time going through school. I may be prejudiced, but I thought our town was a very progressive little town. Ours was a consolidated school, which meant that we had a school district in which all the little country schools would send their junior high and high school kids from the surrounding countryside. There were about four or five little one-room schoolhouses in the countryside.

I never went to a one-room schoolhouse. I was born and raised in the town of Colo, which was blessed with the consolidated school system. We therefore went through grades one through twelve right there in Colo. There, all the grades were in the same building. When the WPA came in during the 1930s, our school built a new building with a gym in the basement. It was a pretty good-sized building. We also had an auditorium with a stage, a home economics' room, and even extra classroom space.

In my early school years, there were fifteen or twenty in my class. The grades were in separate rooms, except for the seventh and eighth grades. Seventh and eighth graders would go to an assembly room, and then go to other rooms for their classes—literature, English, math, and so on.

I had a neighbor who was the same age as myself. We met in first or second grade. His name was Stan Squires. His dad had an aviary where they had bees and processed honey, which they hauled all over the country. His dad was the "honeyman." Stan's granddad actually owned the aviary; his name was "Honey" Hall. At least that was his nickname. My friendship with Stan lasted all through high school, and even into World War II. In fact, we got together in Europe after the war was over as part of the Army of Occupation.

The two of us, Stan and I, had more darn fun on that little Lake Veva. Stan had found an old honey vat that was made of copper, which was about four feet by six feet. He dragged it downhill and into the pond, and it floated like a boat. We pretended that we were exploring the Isthmus of Panama, discovering new lands. We were Columbus! We were explorers. And we just had a great time. But we never were pirates; we were always the "good guys!" Of course, we might have had to fight the pirates off, but then, we were super-powerful. And it all happened on three acres—on little Lake Veva!

Then in the wintertime, because the pond was so shallow, it would freeze over very solid. We would ice skate on the pond, and high school kids would come over, and we'd have hockey games with teams. The pond was great fun.

The neighbor who lived between Stan's place and ours was a carpenter. He was a man who "didn't need any help." He had a 1926 Buick Touring Car with a canvas top. It had four doors and a long wheelbase. He'd drop the top and use his Buick to carry his ladders to the neighbors' farms, where he'd build barns. He'd set up the frames. In those days, the barns were always timber-framed. He'd use 6" x 6" and 4" x 4" lumber to build the frame for a new barn. He would just frame them, then the neighbors would all come in for a barn raising. All the neighbors were amateur carpenters and they'd all pitch in and do whatever was necessary. And away they'd go. They'd end up having a real party. They'd finish the barn off. Sometimes, they wouldn't get it entirely done in one day, but they would come back and work until they finished the barn.

To raise a barn, they would start by lifting the whole doggone wall into position. It would have no siding on it; it was just a skeleton made out of heavy timbers. They then used props to push up the first side until it was vertical. They'd use longer props as they raised it higher.

Finally, as they got it vertical, they used props at both ends to hold it up and keep it plumb. Then they would lift the second side and join it with the first side. They would then have a corner, which would give strength and stability to their work. They would then put the other two sides up, and lo and behold, they had a barn framed. Next came the horizontal siding. For siding they used 1" x 12" barn boards, which were nailed to the horizontal nailers.

The barns would generally give a little bit in a windstorm, and then spring back. They were very rugged. Very few barns blew down. The biggest threat to barns was lightning. A lightning strike would burn a barn down in a hurry. You stored hay up in the haymow. When lightning would strike, it would ignite anything that would kindle. If you had a load of loose hay in your haymow, when lightning struck, boom! That thing went off!

My mother's barn down in Maxwell was struck by lightning. So, they built a new barn and it, too, was struck and burned by lightning. Later, when I got back from the army, as a member of the volunteer fire department, I witnessed other barns burn down. Most of our calls were to go to a barn that was burning down. When we got to the fire, we mostly directed our efforts to saving the outbuildings.

We entertained ourselves in many different ways. We had one of the first radios. My dad rigged it up with a battery charger so that it would operate off of a storage battery and the charger. It was an American Bosch radio. The base the radio sat on was a cabinet for the storage of records or sheet music. My mother played the piano and was a singer, so she had sheet music and records.

On the radio, my favorite shows were *Amos and Andy*, *The Shadow*, *I Love a Mystery*, *Jack Armstrong*, *Little Orphan Annie*, and many others. On Saturday nights, my parents would take the eggs into town to trade them for groceries, and they would give us a nickel or a dime, and we would go to the movies. On Thursday, Friday, and Saturday, the movies were the same. Then on Sunday, they would have the number one movies.

In Colo there was a rather unique movie theater. It was a vacant lot between two stores. The merchants subsidized the movies there, but we still had to pay a nickel or a dime to "get in" to see the movie. Most of the movies there were serials about the marines. They were always in black and white. *The Hound of the Baskervilles* was one movie that we saw. We didn't get the first-run movies in our open-air theater. And if it rained, too bad! You had to leave. There was no raincheck.

When I was in about fifth or sixth grade, we played playground football. I tackled a guy and chipped one of my bottom front teeth. It was right in the center of my mouth; I just knocked a little chip off it. But the tooth is still in my mouth and still does its work.

And we played checkers and Chinese checkers.

Then in 1939, Hitler's German troops invaded Poland. Storm clouds were gathering. To meet the threat, Congress passed the *National Defense Act*. President Roosevelt told Congress and the nation, "I want planes and tanks to prepare our country to protect our shores. "

Then on December 7, 1941, the Japanese bombed Pearl Harbor. America declared war on Japan, and then when Germany declared war on us, we declared war on Germany and Italy. We were then at war with all three of the Axis powers.

Yet during the Depression years, as difficult as life was, few people gave up. Most pulled together. When there was a disaster on a family farm, such as death or serious injury, all the neighbors would come in and do whatever was necessary to keep the farm operation going—like doing the plowing, planting, or harvesting. If a farmer couldn't keep his farm up due to something serious, the neighbors would pitch in. The neighbors would all converge with their own tractors and equipment and make their contributions. Such disasters brought together a lot of people, who until then were just going along on their own. The neighbors would say, "It's not going to happen in our town; we're going to help!" It was a spirit that people had. It was an opportunity to show the world that they could keep their neighbor's family going.

Remember Pearl Harbor. And "God Bless America!"

CHAPTER 4

I ALWAYS SAID, GENE AUTRY LED ME TO THE CONVENT.

- SISTER FELICIA SCHLECHTER, OSF -
(Born March 9, 1929)

My name is Sister Felicia Schlechter. I am a member of the Order of St. Francis of Assisi. I am ninety-one years old. I was born on March 9, 1929.

My adopted mother's name was Kathleen Halligan. She was from Moorland, Iowa. She first taught school in Iowa, and then she went to teach in South Dakota, and that's how she came to meet Dad.

My dad, August J. Schlechter, was from South Dakota. He did three years of high school in Polo, South Dakota, and then finished up his fourth year at a Catholic school in Dyersville, Iowa. While in Dyersville, he got his technical training as an electrician. He then returned to South Dakota. He worked there for about three years, and lived on a farm.

My mother had been dating another man who wasn't a Catholic, and she broke off with him. Then she met my dad. They were both musically inclined. They both played instruments. Dad played the violin and the clarinet. Mom played the piano.

They found that they both liked dancing, so they went dancing in Yankton, South Dakota where a young Lawrence Welk had his band, and they danced to the music of his band. Mom would talk about that every once in a while.

Then, Dad found this place in Rockwell City, Iowa. By this time, my parents were married, and they moved to Iowa. He worked at any job he could find to earn some money. My father had a lot of jobs. I don't know how he kept it all afloat. But he did. He worked for somebody for a while as a mechanic. At the same time, he also shucked corn. But as I mentioned above, Dad was an electrician, but just a budding electrician. He worked for another gentleman for a while who had an electric shop or business. When he began, he was rather like an apprentice, but after he got good, he helped wire the whole county. And he did all this while he farmed.

Then, when my parents found that they couldn't have children, they decided to adopt. I'm an adopted child. I was born on March 9, 1929, and I think I was adopted in that same year. My sister, Joanne, was adopted about a year-and-a-half later. We were adopted out of St. Monica's home for unwed mothers and orphans in Sioux City, Iowa.

It was run by the Benedictine Sisters. I did not find out that I had been adopted until after I entered the convent, years later. For years, I thought I had dreamed about a nun coming down the stairs, carrying a child. Years later, I found out that it wasn't a dream. The child that was being brought down the stairs was my sister, Joanne. My parents were picking up my sister, and I was with them.

I was raised in Rockwell City, Iowa, which is about twenty-six miles west of Fort Dodge and ninety-six miles east of Sioux City.

Our house was situated on a small, twelve-acre farm with a big pond. From the front of our home, just across our pond, we had a lovely view of a city park. Our house was a three-story house, with a third story that was a spacious attic. There were three bedrooms, a bathroom, and a linen closet on the second floor. The first floor had a large kitchen adjacent to a half-bath, a dining room, and a very long living room with a working fireplace. French doors separated the living room from the sun room, which faced east. And there was also a small room that we called the "cold room" because it wasn't heated. The rest of the house was heated by a furnace. The registers could be kept closed so as to save on fuel. When we weren't using the dining room, Dad would close it off and we didn't heat it. We needed to save that fuel; times were tight. We had faucets in the house from which we got hard water. Upstairs we had a bathtub, and downstairs we had a half-bath. That hard water came from the city. But we also had a big cistern outside the house. We'd catch rainwater. That would be the soft water that we used to do the laundry.

There were a number of rooms in the basement, which had a smooth stone floor throughout. We roller skated from room to room.

One room was the furnace room. Our furnace burned coal. We had to shovel that into the furnace when we needed heat. Later, we got a stoker, which also burned coal.

Adjacent to the furnace room was the coal room. I can recall that one time, Dad sent us out along the railroad tracks to pick up the coal that had dropped off the coal cars. It was hard to keep everything together at times.

The laundry room was also in the basement. There was a wood-burning stove in the laundry room, where my mother would heat water in a large oval copper tub for washing clothes. At first we had washboards, then we had a washing machine in there. It had a ringer that you operated by hand. You turned the rollers with your elbow grease. You had to turn the handle to make the rollers move. Then, you took the clothes outside to hang them on the clothesline. In the wintertime, they would freeze-dry out there. Then for a while, we had a Delco motor in the laundry room that provided electricity for the house. I think it ran the washing machine and other things that needed electricity. Later, after Dad wired the house, we had electricity. Dad helped wire the county with the REA. So, I'm sure we got it first. Then he went out and wired for the county.

There was also a separator in the laundry room. We milked three cows, so we always had to separate our milk from the cream. You'd put cream in one pail, and milk in the other. Then we made our butter out of our cream, and our cottage cheese out of the skim milk. So, you'd get skim milk, whole milk, and cream from that separator.

Then too, we kept our icebox in the laundry room. At the time, we had an ice house in our barnyard. During winter, a lot of ice would form on our pond. Two or three men would cut the ice up into huge two- or three-foot squares and then get them from the pond up to the ice house, which was full of sawdust. The sawdust helped keep the ice from melting. I don't know how exactly they did it; it was up quite a steep hill. They had to somehow drag it up the hill. Then when we needed ice for the icebox, they would cut off a chunk and bring it in. At the time, we had no refrigerators; only iceboxes to keep our food cold. So, there was a stove, an icebox, a separator, and a washing machine in that laundry room.

Down in the basement, next to the laundry room, was another room where we stored all our food. There were two big crocks with sauerkraut that we made from cabbage.

And finally, in another room, we had two incubators where we hatched baby chicks. We had perhaps one hundred baby chicks in those incubators. That room was near the furnace room, so it was warm.

Our farm was about one half mile from Highway 20, in Calhoun County. Our farm was about a half mile outside the Rockwell City limits. We were right on old Highway 20.

An old brick factory had previously occupied the land where we had our home place. At the time Mom and Dad bought it, there was a nice house and a nice big dairy barn on the land. By that time, it had been plotted off as a small farm. I don't know when the brick factory was taken down, but it was all gone by that time. But every year, my sister and I would have to go out and pick up the bricks that came up out of the ground. If you've ever been to Wisconsin, you know how glacial rocks work their way up and out of the ground. So, we had to pick up bricks, but my dad was very thoughtful. He bought us a wonderful coaster wagon which we used to collect rocks, and with which we also played. Dad did some farming on the side. We had a lot of chickens, cows, hogs, and sheep. We raised sheep, and for a while, he raised turkeys, too.

Because we always milked three cows, and because there were heifers and other animals on the farm, there was always a lot of farm work to do. Plus, we had pastures where we grew alfalfa and rye. So, we had a lot of harvesting to do. He had to cut the hay, and then put it in the big haymow. We had a big, beautiful dairy barn.

At the front of the barn, the hay would be pulled up into the mow. At first, the hay was just thrown in. Later, they baled it before they put it in the haymow. But there was also an incline or a driveway at the back of the barn. That driveway went right up to the big barn's haymow. You could drive the tractor and hayrack with a load of hay right into the haymow.

As I mentioned, my dad was a mechanic. He also worked for a garage. And while he was there, he cut down an International truck to make it into a tractor. We used that tractor to pull the mower, to pull the hayrack, and to do all our farm work. I learned to drive on it.

As I mentioned above, between the city park and our home, we had a big pond. It was fed by two springs. My dad utilized the water to irrigate a garden which he had made to sell produce. It was like a farmers' market. I know he raised potatoes, because he dusted the potatoes, and we had to go out and pick off the potato bugs. I recall him raising all kinds of vegetables and melons.

Later on, Dad sold the pond to the city, and got three acres of land in return. The pond was also about three acres. The city then turned the pond into a swimming pool. In the 1930s or 1940s, the city had dredged the pond, and created a large hill along our property. High school kids would then drive up on that hill, but it took a quick turn. Once in a while, their cars would slide off the side of the hill, and end up in our driveway. But that hill was really used by the city for sledding and tobogganing, as well as a lot of other things.

We were about a football field's length away from railroad tracks and a coal dock. The coal dock was a place where they would bring in cars loaded with coal. An iron grill or grate with openings, perhaps eight inches square, covered a hole in the ground. The track ran over that iron grillwork, and they would empty a train car loaded with coal over the grate, and the coal would fall through the grate into the hole below. The coal would then be lifted by an elevator up into a three-story high tower, which sat next to the tracks. In those days, train engines burned coal to make steam. The train car immediately behind the engine, was the car that carried the coal that would be burned by the engine. It was called the "tender." The coal tower was there to fill the tenders with coal. The engine would stop with the tender next to the coal tower. The tower had a door, and below the door was a coal chute. Once the tender was parked below the chute, the door above the chute would be opened, and the coal would slide down the chute from the tower into the tender.

Many times, the trains would come in to the coal docks and hobos would get off the trains there to avoid getting arrested if they were caught riding the trains into town. There was a hobo camp where they got off, down in the ravine, between the railroad tracks and the siding. They'd build a fire down in the ravine, and they would eat together. My sister and I never went to the hobo camp.

During the Depression, a lot of men did not have jobs. Many were often in desperate straits. They were rather callously called "bums" or "hobos" at the time. Those men would jump trains and travel all over the United States, trying to find a job. A lot of them came to our house, looking for food. My mother would always feed them. She would give them sandwiches. Sometimes, my sister and I would sit out on the stoop and eat sandwiches with them.

One time, the "King of the Hobos" came to our door. There was always a "King of the Hobos" in Iowa. Every year, there was a certain guy who'd be made the king. He came to our place. At the time, we had three cows, because we always milked cows. He wanted milk—not cold milk, warm milk. So, because he was the king, we had to go out and milk the cows so he could have warm milk. He was very happy to have it. It was kinda funny that he stopped at our place, but I guess we were the "marked" place. A lot of these men stopped at our place. Like I said, my mom always fed them. It was the Depression: You had to help people. These men were all men who had left their families to find jobs.

One winter, we suspected one of these men went into our barn to get warm, and once inside he lit a match, perhaps to light a cigarette, and in the process, he burned our barn down. We didn't actually see anybody burn down our barn, but that was our deduction. That's what we believed happened. We believed it because their camp was so close to our house, and there was nothing else to start a fire in the barn. It just made sense. It was cold weather. It was a big, beautiful, blue dairy barn, sitting right there, filled with lots of hay. In the fire, we lost our dog, and some chickens, but not our main animals.

My dad then found and bought a smaller, older barn, and hauled it in. They hauled it from the small farm where it had been onto our acreage. But it was never the same again. It didn't quite fit. The incline, or driveway, was still there, but it no longer served its purpose. The sheep, however, would still walk up that driveway, but there was quite a drop off along the right-hand side of the incline. Sometimes the sheep would just fall off and break their legs. That always irritated my dad, because there was no insurance coverage for that. They'd just go over the edge and break their legs. They'd fall into the manure pit area. I don't know why the sheep went up the incline, or why they didn't just go back down. Sheep are funny animals. There might have been grass growing on the incline. The incline was next to the barn, but it no longer had any purpose.

We had the sheep for their wool. We did a lot of shearing of sheep. They'd do it every year, in September or October, when it was still warm. We'd come home from school, and we'd see them out there. They used something that looked like a razor. They'd cut the wool off in strips, just as if you were shaving. They'd sheer off long strips of wool with that razor. Dad had a place to sell that wool and make money on it. Then, we'd still have the sheep to have their babies. We had a lot of lambs that we had to feed by hand. I never did any of the shearing; it was always done by the men. We'd just come home from school and see them doing it.

In the 1930s, the dust storms came. I remember I was about four years old at the time. I was outside, and my mother came out and grabbed me. The dust that was coming from Nebraska and Oklahoma was really heavy. You couldn't see anything. She grabbed me, and took me in the house, and we stayed in the house. We didn't go out again because the dust was just terrible.

My sister Joanne and I went to Catholic grade school. To get there, we'd walk along the railroad right-of-way, past the coal docks. We'd go past the coal dock, and if a train was just standing there, we'd crawl under it to get to the other side. If we had walked all the way to either end of the train, it would have been another quarter mile, and we would have been late for school. We had to be there by eight o'clock in the morning. So, we'd crawl under the train to get to the gravel road, and we'd then go another seven or eight blocks to school.

In Rockwell City, my sister and I went to St. Francis Catholic School. The school was part of our parish. I don't know how the building ended up as a Catholic school. It had earlier been an old three-story courthouse, which had been moved. The new courthouse was in the center of town.

On the upper story of the old courthouse, we had the high school. On the second story, they had a chapel and the nuns' quarters. On the first floor, there were three classrooms and a music room. There were back and front entrances; I only recall going in through the front entrance. The classroom nearest to the stairway to the second floor accommodated three classes: the first, second, and third grades. Across the hall, the room was used for the fourth and fifth grades. It looked out at the black walnut and red hawthorn trees, and at a ditch with a lot of water in its lower part. I recall my fourth-grade teacher went into that ditch with her ice skates, and had all the kids bring their ice skates, and we skated there.

On the same side of the building as that fourth-grade room was the music room, where they had choir practice and gave music lessons. Then on the other side, facing south, was the sixth, seventh, and eighth-grade room. There was no kindergarten. I started there in first grade. As I said, the high school was upstairs on the third floor. I can remember that at the end of the school day we had to stay in our classroom.

The big kids would come bounding down the stairs, and we would get run over! Including the high school kids, I don't think we ever had more than ninety kids in the school.

One special memory I have of that school occurred when I was in fourth grade. We all went down to the basement, which later became the lunch room, and listened on the radio as Eugenio Pacelli was being installed as Pope Pius XII. That's my big memory.

And I can remember our eighth-grade nun. We had always had the Sisters of Mercy before. Then for eighth grade, the Franciscan sisters came. My teacher was a short, stocky, but very vibrant woman, Sister Marcia Risach. One day she gave a vocation talk, and at the end told us that if we wanted to be a priest or a sister to go home and tell our parents. So, at noon, I went home and told them I wanted to be a sister. My mother started to cry, and my dad just said, "Eat your lunch!" Then, after my junior year of high school, I visited the convent and again said I wanted to be a sister. My mom said, "Why don't you wait until after your senior year?" So I did. That summer, I detasseled corn for two weeks until I earned enough money for my dowry.

We had a radio at home. We listened to it all day long. We listened to news in the morning, at noon, at suppertime, and at 10 p.m. In between, my dad loved to listen to what was then called "mountain music." Now they call it Country and Western. It was broadcast from Yankton. We also listened to WHO in Des Moines with "Dutch" Reagan, who later became President Ronald Reagan. He was our sports announcer.

We listened to a lot of the soap operas as well, such as *Ma Perkins*, *Backstage Wife*, and *Stella Dallas*. And we listened to mystery stories like *The Shadow* and *Lights Out*. We'd listen to *Lights Out* at eleven o'clock at night. It was a mystery show. It was supposed to be scary. And then, there were afternoon shows, like *Jack Armstrong* and *Captain Midnight*.

And we played games. In the house, Mom and Dad taught us checkers and Chinese checkers. We did a lot of jigsaw puzzles, and my sister and I played a lot of elementary card games, such as Old Maid and Hearts. Then, when we went outside, we played ball. At school, we played "baseball" with a big, round, rubber ball, which we hit with our hand rather than with a bat. And we played tag and hide-and-go-seek. A lot of times, we'd just lie on the grass and watch the stars, or look up at the sky and find images in the clouds.

We had a theater in town, so we went to the movies. It was a dime for us. When mom went with us, after the movie we would go next door to Joe's Candy Kitchen. When she wasn't with us, we'd stay at the movie all afternoon and watch a double feature, with a cartoon and a newsreel. In those days, there was no television, so we'd get our news from the newsreels. The one movie that I remember best was a Gene Autry movie, "South of the Border." It was on an afternoon. And I went with my sister, Joanne. I loved all the Gene Autry movies. In this one, there was a scene where he had gone back to Mexico to find this girl he loved. He was in love with a Mexican girl, and there was a scene where he went into the chapel in the mission church and saw her kneeling there in a veil of white in the candle light. She had gone into the convent. So, he decided to return to the United States. After that, I always said, Gene Autry led me to the convent. I think it was then that I decided to be a sister. There was a popular song called "South of the Border." It was the theme song of that movie. I'll always remember the one line from the song, "There in a veil of white by candlelight, she knelt to pray. . . ."

CHAPTER 5

THE RADIO HAD WIRES WITH ALLIGATOR CLIPS THAT ATTACHED TO THE BATTERY POSTS. TO RECHARGE THE BATTERY, YOU HAD TO TAKE IT TO TOWN.

- MAURY MARTIN -
(Born July 7, 1928)

I was the youngest of seven children. We lived for most of my young life around North Liberty, Iowa. We rented farms. We did not own them. We probably couldn't afford to buy them. At that time, it seemed as if many farms were owned by the insurance companies. I think they had foreclosed on many folks, and they ended up owning a lot of farms. We rented three or four of the farms on which we lived from insurance companies. We moved a lot. In fact, we probably moved every three or four years.

Of all the places we lived, the place we lived longest was near North Liberty. We rented a 240-acre farm there. In those days, a 240-acre farm was a big operation. The insurance companies always wanted to sell you the farm. We probably should have bought that big farm. It fit right in with our big family. I had three brothers and three sisters, and I was the youngest. And according to all of them, I was spoiled. And maybe, I was. I don't know.

With seven kids and my mom and dad, there were nine of us at the kitchen table. My mother, bless her heart, worked very hard in front of the Home Comfort kitchen stove to feed us. I would say that, because we lived on the farm, we lived quite well.

It seemed as if food was always plentiful. We always had enough food on the table. That was one good thing about farming. But income was very short, slight. Our income was basically from milk. I think we lived on the "milk check." If it wasn't for the milk check, I think we'd have starved to death. During the time we lived on the 240-acre farm, we always milked anywhere from fifteen to twenty milk cows. We had no electricity at the time, so everything was done pretty much by hand, including the separating. We used hand-turned separators to separate the cream from the skimmed milk.

We always also had lots of chickens and lots of eggs. So, we always had eggs to eat and sell. During those years, the egg market always seemed to hold pretty well. Eggs were a good commodity. We also had a lot of hogs. Then of course, we grew corn and beans for crops. We always had a rotation: corn, then beans, and then maybe oats or hay. We had a Chevy truck—a 1924 model as I recall—that had a grain box on it. We used it to haul oats. I can remember my brother scooping oats into the box on the truck, and then he'd take them somewhere, and we'd sell them.

Our entertainment was basically the radio. Our radio was powered by a battery. That radio battery was just like a car battery. It sat behind the radio. The radio had wires with alligator clips that attached to the battery posts. To recharge the battery, you had to take it to town. You'd leave it at the garage for an hour or so, and then it would be ready to go. Once it was charged, you took it back home, put it behind the radio, attached the clips, and away it would go. It worked well, and would run the radio quite a while. I'm not quite sure exactly how long, but for hours. Of course, we had to be very careful that we didn't run the battery down. The radio simply had to work if there was going to be a Joe Lewis fight.

My dad was particularly insistent that we be especially careful not to run the battery down around the time of any Joe Lewis fight. As kids, we listened to a lot of what I would call "kids' programs," like *Jack*

Armstrong, Little Orphan Annie, and *The Shadow.* Later in the evening, the grownups would listen to shows like *Fibber McGee and Molly* and stuff like that.

I can still remember what a typical week was like in those days.

Monday was always wash day. With no electricity, the washing machine was powered by a gas-powered Briggs and Stratton motor. That motor was a little motor with a starter pedal. You stepped down on the pedal and hopefully the motor would start. Sometimes it started and sometimes it didn't. But often, when my mother tried to start it, it would seem to "fight back," and my mother would be unable to get it started. She'd try to get it going, but when she couldn't, she would call in one of my brothers. They were pretty good mechanics and were pretty good at fixing the washing machine and keeping it running. The motor was connected to the washing machine with belts. The washing machine was a Maytag, if I recall. The motor sat right under the tub. The belt ran the agitator in the washer. It was a pretty good setup . . . when it worked. Because it was a gasoline engine, there was a ten or twelve-foot hose that took the exhaust fumes from the motor in the basement out the window.

Tuesday seemed to be a baking day. Wednesday and Thursday were gardening days. Friday always seemed like a cleaning day. It was the day you cleaned the house.

Saturday was "go to town" day; it was the day when we bought staples, like flour. We always bought flour in a fifty-pound bag because my mother really did a lot of baking. She was very talented when it came to making breads and buns, and other fresh stuff like that. And if we were really lucky, when we went to town on Saturday, we might get to see a movie in Iowa City. In those days, you could go to a movie for ten or twenty cents—but that was pretty big money.

Sunday was church day. My mother was pretty strict with us kids about going to church. My dad, however, didn't go to church. He'd drop mom and us kids off at church, and then he would go up to the garage in town and they would pitch horseshoes. Pitching horseshoes was a big thing in those days. Then, when church was over, he'd come back and pick us up.

Sunday was a rather relaxing day. We didn't work that hard, but we still had to milk the fifteen to twenty cows. They still had to be milked by hand, twice a day. That was a very important thing. Three or four of us did most of the milking. That included my mother, my dad, and two or three of us kids. The cows, in general, were very docile, except the Holsteins who always wanted to kick us. So, we put something on them that we called "kickers." That was a chain-type thing that kept them from putting their feet in the milk bucket. Now, we didn't always throw the milk away if a cow put her foot in the bucket; we'd just strain the milk. We then stored the milk in ten-gallon cans, and put the cans in what was supposed to be cool water. The milk was picked up at our place by the milkman with his truck. He took the ten-gallon cans to Sidwell Dairy in Iowa City. They processed the milk and sold it in quarts. The people in town had a milkman, who if I recall, delivered every day, or at least three or four times a week. But that "milk check" was an important thing for our income during the troubled times of the 1930s.

While we lived on that big farm, I went to school for eight years in a one-room schoolhouse. One thing that was really different was that my older sister taught there while I was in the seventh and eighth grades. In those days, a person who wanted to become teacher could go to a teachers' college, and get a certificate to teach school. That is what my sister had done. She was a very good teacher. Later on, after she got married, she taught at the university, and became a professor. She got her doctor's degree in education. Our school was a pretty nice school. It even had electricity. Of course, it had outdoor toilet facilities—one for the boys, and one for the girls. It was a very adequate school.

When my sister was teaching at our one-room school, she always got her check from the president of the school board. He was just another farmer who lived in the area. One day, when I was in seventh or eighth grade, this president brought a bunch of switches to school. He told my sister that she had to use the switches on some of the kids, because "they had been picking on his kid." That wasn't true. She refused to do what he wanted, and he said that he wasn't going to give her her check. She came home crying and told my dad what had happened. That didn't sit well with my dad. My sister was family, and no one picked on the family. So, Dad jumped in his car and drove over to the farm where this fellow lived. The president was in the barn, and he told my dad that he wasn't going to give my sister her check until she used the switches on some of the kids. He then went back into the barn, got his pitchfork, and came back out. My dad was a pretty big guy. He went about six-foot-three and weighed about 240 pounds. He told the guy, "Either you're going to give me my daughter's check, or you're going to eat that pitchfork a little at a time." The president finally decided to give Dad the check, but said, "This isn't fair. Those kids need to be switched." My dad said, "She'll decide who needs to be switched." So, Dad came home with my sister's check. Dad was a great family man. He stood up for his family.

And there was another good thing about living on that farm. There was a trolley line that ran from Cedar Rapids to Iowa City, which was a distance of roughly twenty-eight miles. We called it the "Interurban." It ran on a single track, along Highway 218. It carried both passengers and freight.

The Interurban wasn't a real passenger train. It was an electric trolley line. It was just a one-car trolley that ran on electricity, supplied by overhead wires. Attached to the roof of the trolley was an arm that reached up and made contact with those electrical wires.

It ran on a schedule, but if you stopped anywhere along the tracks and held up your hand, the trolley would stop and pick you up. From our place, you could ride to Iowa City for about twenty cents. It was about ten miles from our place near North Liberty to Iowa City. We'd go down and wait along Highway 218 for it to come, and it would stop and pick us up. Many times, when we were in high school, the motorman would stop and give us a free ride to Iowa City, and we'd save our twenty cents. What we saved, we could foolishly spend on something else. In those days, you sort of trusted everybody; you didn't worry about people molesting kids. If there really were "good old days," I guess those were good old days.

When the Interurban got to the end of the track in Cedar Rapids, there was no turn around. The motorman would just take the controller, go to the other end of the car, and put it in place. Then you'd go in that direction. When it got to Iowa City, they could turn around. They'd go uptown, and make a loop around the block. Then, they'd be going back the other way. In Iowa City there was a depot where passengers could wait to get on.

As I mentioned, the Interurban also hauled freight. It hauled quite a bit of coal between Cedar Rapids and Iowa City.

One of the things we did for fun was to go to the University of Iowa football games. You could ride the Interurban and it would take you very close to the football stadium. The football stadium was in the same place that it is now, but in those days, it accommodated only about twenty-five thousand fans. And there was what they called the "knothole section," where kids could go and see a football game for twenty-five cents or less. We'd go and sit in the knothole seats, which probably held five or six thousand kids—high school and grade school kids. It was a real good deal. Iowa Saturday football in those days was a big, big deal. We went to a lot of football games. Those were the days of Nile Kinnick. They later named the stadium after him. In those days, Iowa had big rivalries with Ohio State and Notre Dame. Today, the stadium has been expanded to hold from seventy-five to eighty thousand fans.

As kids, we had a form of entertainment that was pretty unusual. We played "barrel rolls." We'd take a thirty or sixty-gallon barrel, with the top cut out, and you'd stand on the barrel, barefooted and balanced. You'd then roll the barrel with your feet. You'd walk on the barrel. We had a game where we'd try to knock each other off the barrels. We'd get pretty good at balancing ourselves on the barrels. And we rolled them all around the yard. You could turn by just shifting your weight on the barrel. It was a lot of fun.

Then too, from the time we were ten or twelve years-old, we always had bikes.

When it got dark, we would entertain ourselves outside by playing hide-and-go-seek. Inside the house, we'd play ping pong on the dining room table.

Every town, in that era, had fast-pitch softball. The towns would have teams. The teams would get together and play each other, often times on Sunday during the afternoon. It was entertainment. A lot of the teams had their names and the name of their sponsors on their uniforms. It was a big thing.

The house that we lived in in North Liberty was, at one time, quite a fancy house. It had five bedrooms and a bath upstairs. Downstairs, we had four or five pretty big rooms.

The house had originally had a central hot water or steam heating system. But by the time we moved in, that system was broken and wouldn't function any longer. I imagine that was because nobody had money to fix it. So, we didn't have central heating. Of course, we had the Home Comfort stove in the kitchen, where all the cooking was done. And we had kerosene heaters. One was in the dining room and the other was in the parlor. They weren't teeny little things; they were pretty good size stoves. They did a pretty good job of heating those rooms, and those were big rooms, even by today's standards.

The heat from the first floor didn't get to the upstairs where all the sleeping rooms were. The only way we ever made it more comfortable was to take an iron—like you'd heat on the kitchen stove to press clothes—and wrap it in paper or something. It didn't get hot enough to burn, but you could put your feet over it and it would keep your feet pretty warm. Otherwise, the upstairs was unheated, even in winter time.

For water, we had a windmill that pumped water from a well. To collect the water, we had a big concrete supply tank, which provided the water for the hogs and the cattle. I don't know how much water that big concrete tank held, but it was big. The windmill pumped the water from the well to fill that concrete tank.

At one time, this big house had a water system. But when we lived there, that system was shot and didn't work. What they had was a storage barrel in the attic. There were steps going up to the attic, which was like a third floor. You could walk around up in the attic. That barrel would provide running water for the kitchen and the bath. But it no longer worked when we lived there. We had to carry the water to the house from the windmill. Our drinking water came from an outside well that had a pump. You pumped up the water, and that's what you took into the house for drinking and cooking water. I always said, I was six or seven years old before I realized my name wasn't "Get water!" or, "Get wood!" We were always getting water for the house, or wood for the wood stove. If someone wanted to take a bath, you had to get water from outside and carry it up the stairs. It was an interesting life, and it certainly was different from today.

We lived on the North Liberty farm from probably 1935 until 1942. In 1941 we got electricity. That was through the REA—the Rural Electrification Association. And that was a really big thing. We had no wall switches, just pull chains. The electricity was only in the house, not in the barn or in any of the other buildings. That came a bit later.

I'll always remember the telephones. We had the old-type telephone that you cranked. We had a party line. There were usually four of five people on your party line. I recall that our ring was "long, two shorts, and a long." When one person's phone rang on the line, everybody else's phone rang. And I think everybody on the line listened to everybody else's conversations! Having a telephone in those days was quite a thing.

For me, nothing is more amazing than how phones have changed over the last ninety years. I compare the cell phones we have today with those old phones that hung on the wall with a crank on the side and their big batteries. The old telephone batteries were different from the auto-type battery we used in our old radios. They were similar to today's modern flashlight batteries. The old telephone batteries were about twelve inches long and bigger-around than today's flashlight batteries. They seemed to last a long time, but unlike today's cell phone batteries, you could not recharge them. Each telephone had two of these batteries. To replace them, you'd open the front part of the wooden telephone. You could get replacements at Sears Roebuck and many other stores.

We always had horses on the farm. We always had a good team of horses. My dad always used the horses to plant the corn. The corn was planted so that you could row it crossways—so it could be cultivated in both directions.

As I mentioned above, we also milked cows. The milk cows always wanted to come into the barn when it was time to milk them, because that's when they got fed. All our milk cows had names that we had given them, like Ole Pep. Ole Pep would come up to us when we came out to get the cows. When they came in, we hooked them to the stanchion, and they had a little feed trough at the front of the stanchion. Boy, they liked to come in and get something to eat. And they ate a lot of feed every day to produce milk. Many farms that had electricity had electric milkers that they would put on the cows. We didn't have electricity, so we did our milking manually. We milked them by hand twice a day, and you had to be there morning and night. And if you went somewhere visiting, you started home by 3:30, so you could be home in time to do the evening milking.

Later we did have tractors. We bought a new International F-20 tractor with steel wheels. We did a lot of farming with that tractor. We later had an RCT. Then, when Ford came out with smaller tractors, we got a Ford. And we also had an old truck that I will always remember. We always had quite a bit of equipment to do the farming.

On this farm, we really had two sets of buildings. We had a second set of buildings about a quarter mile away. That's where the hired man lived, before we moved there. He had lived in that second set of buildings.

We had the typical buildings, like the big barn with stanchions for ten or twenty cows, which we used to milk them. We always had a big machine shed, and we always had four or five corn cribs. We were raising eighty acres of corn, which was a big amount then, so we needed bins where we could store the corn.

We always had a hired man who would come in the fall. He stayed at our place and picked corn for us. He picked by hand. When he picked the ears of corn, he'd throw them in a wagon box. The wagon that he used was always pulled by a horse. (The tractor came later.) I don't know how many bushels that wagon box would hold.

On the wagon, we installed a "bang-board." It was like a plank wall, attached to the box on one side of the wagon with cleats. The hired man would walk along one side of the wagon, picking corn. The bang-board would be on the opposite side of the wagon to make that side of the wagon box higher, so that when he tossed the ears of corn into the wagon, he could do so without looking. If he threw them too high, they'd hit the bang-board and fall back into the wagon box. That way, he wouldn't have to stop and pick up ears of corn that overshot the box.

On the back end of the wagon box, there was what was called a "scoop-board." It was a board, hinged at the bottom so you could fold it down. The back wall of the box was lowered to make it easier to get the corn out of the wagon. He'd use a scoop shovel, and shovel the corn from the corn box up into a corn crib. The corn cribs were about six or eight feet high, and once one got full, he'd have to go to the next one. He'd scoop from the wagon box and throw it into a corn crib. He'd get about a wagonload of corn in the morning and a wagonload of corn in the afternoon. He'd scoop off the first load into the bins at noon, and the second in the evening. He'd come in in the late afternoon with almost another full load of corn in the wagon box. A good corn picker would pick a load of corn in the morning, come in for lunch, and scoop that corn into a corn crib. He'd go out again in the afternoon, and probably pick another load of corn before dark. A scoop shovel looked like a coal shovel, but it was bigger than a coal shovel. They still use them for scooping corn into the grinder.

Our hired man was quite a guy. He came from Kansas, and he came about every year during the seven-year period when we lived on that farm, and worked for us. He was very good and very dependable. He worked with my brothers, who also picked the corn, usually picking a couple of loads of corn a day. He worked hard, and he liked beer. He'd say to my brothers, "This weekend, it would be nice if we could get a picnicker of beer." A "picnicker" was a big bottle of beer. They would get some, and sit out in the barn, and have a beer. He did nothing but pick corn. He didn't help with the milking or anything else, but he did do a lot of corn picking.

We had three or four wagons, and my older brothers would have a wagon out there with a horse pulling it. They got so they could just tell the horse to move up, and the horse would move up a little, and that's the way it went, all across the field.

But the corn, besides being picked, had to be shelled.

Generally, there would be a farmer who owned a "corn sheller." The corn sheller would be mounted on a truck. The farmer would take his truck from farm-to-farm. Then they would lay a "drag" along the bottom of the corn crib. They'd then remove the bottom two or three slats that held the corn in the crib. Next, they'd pull the corn from the crib onto the drag using something that looked like a rake. The drag would then pull the corn to the sheller that was right next to it—just a matter of ten or fifteen feet—and the sheller would then shell the ears of corn. The sheller would separate the kernels of corn from the cob, and send the kernels in one direction, and the cobs in another. You ended up with a pile of cobs in one direction, and shelled corn in another. Then, we'd grind the kernels for feed for the cows, pigs, and chickens. We used cobs to get the fire going in the kitchen stove. Once the cobs dried, they would burn really well. Then once you kindled the fire, you would add wood that you had split for fuel.

Later, we bought a two-row corn picker with one of our neighbors, which ran off the power takeoff on our big tractor. It was a "New Idea Corn Picker." I'll always remember that. We picked a lot of corn with that New Idea Corn Picker. Between the neighbor and us, we owned it. We picked our corn, and the neighbor picked his. It worked pretty well. But we still put in some long, long, long days. The milking started in the morning around five or six o'clock. Then of course, we'd milk again in the evening.

We also had another piece of equipment—a "grinder." We'd grind corn to feed to the cows and the hogs. I think the grinder was called a "Hammer Mill Grinder." It ran off of a belt pulley on the tractor.

In 1942, two of my brothers left the farm to fight in World War II. Because they were farmers, they could have gotten deferments. During the war, food was an essential item, and somebody had to raise the food on the farm. Therefore, the farmer was considered essential to the war effort. For that reason, farmers could get deferred from serving in the military. But my older brothers wanted to join the fight.

One of my brothers, after failing to get into the marines because of his poor eyesight, joined the army and spent three and a half years in the South Pacific. He could never tell us where he was. But he came back alive after four years. My other brother joined the merchant marine.

We always had pets. We had a dog and a pet cow. She was a milk cow, and we could stand on her and ride on her. And I will never forget our pet pig. If the newborn pigs weren't right, my dad would put them down. But we talked him into saving one that couldn't walk. Then after a month or two it recovered, and walked almost perfectly. Every time you went out into the yard where the pigs were, this pig would come running up to you. He was just a pet. He grew up and got to weighing a couple hundred pounds. We kids didn't really want Dad to sell that pig until we found out how much money he would bring. Then, we decided it was okay to sell him.

We always had plenty of cats—especially at milking time.

Our cats were what you would call barn cats. They lived mostly in the barn or in a woodpile. They'd catch mice. When we milked, we'd squirt the milk in the direction of a cat, and the cat would almost stand up on its hind legs to catch the milk. And we always had a pan that we would put some milk in to feed the cats, so they lived pretty good. But they did take care of all the mice. We even had one big female cat who could take care of a rat. When they caught a mouse, they'd bring it back into the barn and be very proud of themselves.

We always stored our gasoline on the farm in big barrels. We had a workshop that was like a little building, and the barrels were outside, around the edge of the workshop. One time, my brother was getting gas to put in the car. We had no electricity, but we had a butane light, and my brother said, "Bring it a little closer, so I can see if this thing is full." You can guess what happened then. We got the fumes too close to the butane light, and the barrel caught on fire and burnt the shed down. It was a pretty good size fire. Somebody said, "The firemen are coming," and I got excited thinking I would see a real firetruck. But when they arrived, all they had was a trailer, pulled behind a wrecker from the old garage. That was the firetruck! And on it were some ladders and other stuff for the volunteer firemen to use. All they really did was work to try to keep the fire from spreading from the shed to any of the other buildings. Fortunately, they were able to do so.

One other story that I should tell you is how I earned the last dollar I needed to buy a Red Ryder BB gun. I had been saving my money to buy a Red Ryder BB gun, but I was still short about a dollar. We were talking one night about the other set of buildings on the farm, and how scary it would be to go down there at night. I said, "It wouldn't be scary. I wouldn't be afraid to go down there, at all." The conversation went on and on, and eventually ended when my three older brothers and one of my sisters said, "We'll each give you a quarter if you go down to the other set of buildings and tie a string to the doorknob of each of the upstairs rooms."

I thought, "Boy, this is an easy way to get the last dollar I need to buy the Red Ryder BB gun out of the Sears Roebuck catalog." They allowed me to take a flashlight, and I headed down the road to the other set of buildings. It was a bit more than a quarter of a mile to get there.

My brothers decided that if they took the short cut through the oat field, they could beat me to the old house, hide in the upstairs, leap out, and scare me. But Dad didn't think that would be fair, and he wouldn't let them do it.

So, down the road I went with my trusty little flashlight, which wasn't very bright, and my ball of string to tie around the upstairs door-knobs. All went well until I got next to the buildings, and then a whole bunch of cows that had been sleeping in a corner jumped up and scared the daylights out of me. But eventually, I got my nerve up, entered the house, went upstairs, tied the string around the doorknobs, and scurried back home at a full run.

My brothers went down and checked, and they found the string on the knobs. And I got my quarters! I then had enough money to order my Red Ryder BB gun from the Sears Roebuck catalog, which I did. And I had a real good time with that BB gun. I've always wondered what would have happened if Dad hadn't stopped them from getting there and hiding before I got there. Dad was very protective of the family. Now, everyone in my family is gone, except me.

Some of the townsfolk thought that it wasn't very "romantic" to live on a farm. We were "just farmers." Farming wasn't respected, as it is today. But life on the farm during those days for us was pretty good. I would say that we as kids had it pretty good during the Depression.

CHAPTER 6

AT THE TIME OF MY PARENTS' DIVORCE, DAD WAS LIVING AT MOLINE'S LECLAIRE HOTEL, WHICH WAS A VERY NICE PLACE IN THOSE DAYS.

- DOROTHY T. DENKHOFF -
(Born August 25, 1924)

I was born on August 25, 1924, so I was about five years old when the Depression hit. After I was born, my parents and I lived for a while in in what had been my maternal grandmother's home, on 22nd Street in Moline, Illinois. My mother, who, had been born in 1902, had been raised there. A second child born in 1906 and a third child born in 1908 both died soon after birth. Then Grandma died after giving birth.

I can recall an early Christmas there. Santa Claus came and left me a little ironing board and iron. Then, I can remember watching from the kitchen as Santa walked down the sidewalk to the alley.

My father's parents, the Tilloisons, lived at 1925 6th Avenue, which is now a "historic home." My father's dad passed away in 1927. Dad's mother rented rooms to three, and later to four, school teachers. She served them breakfast each day: coffee, toast, and the peach-honey jam that she made every year. Two of the teachers were rather special. Miss. Day taught civics and Miss. Spencer taught biology at Moline High School. The others, like Bess Barnett, taught elsewhere.

My parents separated when I was very young. My dad then went to live with his mother on 6th Avenue, and took me along, too. Dad and I were still living there at the time of his mother's death in 1932.

During the time that I lived there, I can remember that an iceman would come along the alley in a Moline Consumers Company horse-drawn wagon. He'd grab an ice block with his big tongs, in the size that you wanted, and carry it from his wagon up to the back porch, and put it in the back of the icebox. I'm not sure how often he came.

The icebox, of course, wasn't very cold. And that may be how I got ptomaine poisoning when I was five years old. After school I ate wieners from that icebox. My temperature rose to 105°. I laid on Grandma's round-back sofa for days while Grandmother Tilloison nursed me.

While I lived there, I can also recall playing with friends at Stephens Square Park, at the east edge of Moline's downtown. It was only about a block away. I can also recall walking to Grant School each day as a young girl, and meeting a classmate along the way at the Knox Funeral Home on 6th Avenue. Her father was an embalmer there. Then, we'd walk up the alleys to school.

My parents' divorce was finally settled in 1934. The courts, at the time, felt a girl should be with her mother. So, I was with my mother during the school year, and with my father in June, July, and August.

My mother remarried in 1940. My stepdad worked for the Rock Island Lines in Silvis, Illinois. But even with my stepdad working, money was tight. After they had married, we moved up to that part of Moline known as Hyland.

We moved into in a large, older home on a corner of 30th Street and 23rd Avenue. It had been my stepdad's boyhood family home. My step-dad had remodeled it and turned it into a duplex. We lived on the west side, and his older brother lived on the east side. Our half of the duplex had two nice size bedrooms. I had a double bed, a dresser, a desk, a chair, and a lamp. His younger brother lived upstairs with his wife. Our home was heated by a coal stoker furnace, which we had to keep filled. Our side of the duplex had the stairway to the attic. There were two partially completed rooms in the attic, which could be lived in. But I'm not sure that they were heated.

There was also a large old barn on the lot, along the alley. A driveway from 30th Street went around behind the house and then exited onto 23rd Avenue. Behind the duplex, there was space to park a couple cars.

Galvin's Grocery Store sat kitty-corner from our home. I can remember charging for groceries there.

My dad was a mechanic. He had his business on the corner of 12th Street and 4th Avenue. He later sold cars in Rock Island for Galbraith Motors. Then he acquired his own dealership. His dealership sold Oldsmobiles, Cadillacs, and LaSalles. His showroom was on 5th Avenue, near 17th Street, next to the Paradise Theater. He set up his used car lot at the southeast corner of 16th Avenue and 6th Street. It was a nice lot. He set it up there because space was lacking next to his 5th Avenue dealership building. Later, he lost his dealership. Oldsmobile wanted him to build a new building, but he felt that building would be too expensive. After that, he sold cars for Lundahl's in Davenport.

At the time of my parents' divorce, Dad was living in Moline's LeClaire Hotel, which was a very nice place in those days. It was really quite a place. It sat at the northwest corner of 19th Street and 5th Avenue.

The LeClaire was fifteen stories high. In front of the hotel, along 19th Street, old-fashioned wooden chairs were set out, where you could sit to relax.

On the ground floor, the lobby faced east toward 19th Street. There were sofas and chairs in the lobby. The restaurant, called the Prime Rib Room, was in the northeast corner. If you looked north out its windows, you could see the old Rock Island Railroad Depot.

The kitchen was in the northwest corner. On the south end of the building, there were three businesses. At the southeast corner, there was a long narrow drug store. It had a fountain, and I think a pharmacy. You could purchase all kinds of things that you might need there. At the southwest corner, there was a little bar called The Jug. Between the drug store and the tavern was a beauty shop that I patronized many times.

The main elevator was in the lobby. It was used by the guests and tenants used to get to their rooms. There was a freight elevator at the back of the hotel, on the West side of the building. That elevator was used for freight, and to move the possessions of the guests or tenants in or out.

Above the lobby was a mezzanine that looked down on the lobby from the north and from the south. It had many tables and chairs where one could sit and write a letter, or sit and read. There were also two spacious rooms; one was at the north end, and the other at the south. The one at the south was the manager's apartment; the one to the north was his office.

Above the mezzanine, if I recall, were seven floors of rooms for overnight guests.

Then, above the floors with the rooms for overnight guests, were at least four floors of apartments for people who "lived permanently" at the LeClaire.

At this time, my dad was living at the LeClaire Hotel on the 11th floor, in Room 1107. I have a photograph in which I am seated at a small table in the small kitchen area of that apartment. You can see a refrigerator situated behind me, by the back door, and to the right of that door was the kitchen counter. The door led to the back hallway and to an elevator. The kitchen space was tight, but ample. Then, after my father remarried, we moved to the 10th floor. That apartment had an extra room and a bath that I used. It was off the long north–south hall that ran the length of the building.

The apartments were long and narrow. All had closets near the entrance. Beyond the closet was a dressing room with hangers for clothes, a dresser, and a bath. The beds were in the living room There were two Murphy beds hidden in the walls that dropped down when you opened the doors that hid them.

As I stated above, when I was young, I lived at the LeClaire during the summers with my dad. Then, as I got older, my dad thought it would be better if I were to spend my summers with my mother.

Finally, on the 15th floor of the LeClaire Hotel was the Top Hat Room. It looked out north over the Mississippi River, and it had a large area for dancing at the north end. The room was used for large parties and dances. More to the southern end, there were tables and chairs, and there was also a kitchen, which served the 15th floor.

While we lived in the LeClaire Hotel, the Prince Castle Ice Cream Store was just across 19th Street. You could get a banana split for nineteen cents, with a whole banana, three scoops of ice cream, and fruit on top. I didn't like the fruit, so I had them substitute chocolate fudge and marshmallow cream (not mere marshmallows!). They served it on a fancy glass dish.

We never went out the front door of the hotel, which faced 19th Street. We always cut through the Jug, the little bar that occupied the southwest corner of the first floor of the hotel. We exited onto 5th Avenue. I remember the Jug's cute little sign. Dad's dealership was roughly kitty-corner from the Jug. West of the Jug, but across an alley, was Len's Grill, with its bowling alley down stairs.

When I spent summers with my dad, I had no babysitters. Dad's car dealership, however, stayed open until nine o'clock. The LeClaire and the Paradise movie theaters were, however, both very close, so he sent me there. The Paradise was next door; the LeClaire was just east, in the next block.

As I remember, they always had a double feature, with a Paramount news short in between. I have memories of seeing *Gone with the Wind*, staring Clark Gable and Vivian Lee. And I loved watching the Shirley Temple movies, as she tap-danced. She was very young. And of course, I never missed a Fred Astaire and Ginger Rogers' movie. I loved how they danced. I have no idea what it cost to have the movies "babysit" me.

The Granada Restaurant was on the corner of 18th Street and 5th Avenue. Right next door was Hugh's. Hugh's was a hole-in-the-wall place where you could buy a hamburger for seven cents.

I can remember always buying Fannie May candies at the little store downtown on 5th Avenue at 16th Street. I'd always go in there for mints.

Then, at the northwest corner of 16th Street and 5th Avenue, across the avenue from Fanny May's, was a special little cigar shop, Hickey Brothers. The men liked to go there for lunch. They sat on little stools at the counter. They served many lunches that the men liked.

Montgomery Ward's was at the southeast corner of 6th Avenue and 15th Street. They've been closed for about forty years, but you can still see their fading sign painted on the cement wall that faces west. J. C. Penney's was at the northeast corner of 17th Street and 5th Avenue. The Moline Public Library was located directly south of Penney's, across 5th Avenue. It faced 17th Street.

And then there was Lagomarcino's Candy Shop and Fountain. It sat just west of 15th Street, on the south side of 5th Avenue. It was wonderful. I would buy ribbon candy, which they only made at Christmastime, and seafoam candy, which was chocolate-covered honeycomb candy. And then there was their small, hard licorice. I loved that, and selfishly wouldn't offer it to anyone else.

And I always liked going to Whitey's Ice Cream Shop to get a waffle cone with two dips. That was always a special treat. And there was another place just down the hill along 16th Street called Corsigilas. It was a restaurant and hangout for high school kids after school.

My first job was at Block and Kuhl Co., a department store on 5th Avenue in Moline, in the beauty department. The New York store was just across the street. It was a nice department store. I also worked at Woolworth's, in the china department. I can still recall the wonderful smell of the baked hams that they sold up front by the door.

My stepdad played baseball for a team called the Hylands. I went to many 4th of July ball-team picnics in the area of King's Orchard, where the new Moline High School was later built.

I can also remember the WWI veterans having a yearly get-together and playing music in front of the LeClaire Hotel at night. And when I was young, I can recall marching in a parade on Memorial Day. We carried flowers—chrysanthemums. We marched across the bridge to the Rock Island Arsenal, stopped, and dropped the flowers in the water. In those days, you could drive straight across the Arsenal bridge to Davenport.

My father was a member of Short Hills Country Club in East Moline, Illinois. When I was young, when he played golf, I always went along and walked the eighteen holes with him. When he would get done, we'd go into the downstairs bar and he would buy me a Shirley Temple cocktail. It was made from ginger ale or 7-UP and grenadine. In those days, they had two slot machines in that bar, and I won a jackpot, and got to keep those winnings.

Then, when I got old enough to play golf, I took lessons. And because my dad had a family membership, I played in some of the club's tournaments. On my eighteenth birthday, my party was at Short Hills, and I still have the birthday card and string of pearls Dad gave me.

When I was sixteen (in 1940), I told him I wanted to learn how to drive. Dad said I would have to sell my bike. He put it up for sale in the window of the showroom. When it sold, I got to drive. I was also taught how to do office work by the woman who worked in his office.

CHAPTER 7

WE HAD A RADIO. IT LOOKED RATHER LIKE A CHEST OF DRAWERS. IT WAS FLOOR MODEL. I TELL MY KIDS, WE USED TO HAVE A FISHBOWL SITTING ON TOP. WE'D WATCH THE FISH SWIM WHILE LISTENING TO THE RADIO, AND THAT WAS OUR TV.

- DONALD D. BECK -
(Born February 8, 1931)

We were a family of five. My mother and dad, two older sisters, and me. We never owned a home; my parents rented all their lives. My dad was a barber. He sometimes had his barbershop in our home; at other times, he would work for someone. I can remember that at one point in time he was working at a state hospital, cutting hair and also doing laundry for the entire hospital for thirty dollars a month. We were living in a house where our rent was twelve dollars per month. When the landlord raised the rent to fifteen dollars, my parents did not want to pay that extra rent, so we moved. We really had nothing while I was growing up. We had no washing machines or other luxuries, like we have now.

I was born in Rest, Kansas. When I was about five, we lived in a small town in southeast Kansas. I can't recall the name of the town. In any event, I outlived the town. But when I was about five, I became ill. There was no nearby hospital. The doctor came to our house. I can't recall his name. He determined that I had pleural pneumonia. He operated on me on our kitchen table, and inserted a rubber tube into my side to drain my lung. After a period of time, when the drainage was ceasing, he pulled it out and put bandages over it. We then moved to another town, and that doctor wasn't around. So, my parents had to change the bandages once a day.

One day, I was playing under our kitchen table. I bumped my side. It really hurt. That night, when Dad changed my bandage, he saw something. It was a part of the rubber hose that had broken off when the doctor pulled it out of my side. My dad then pulled it out and put the bandages back on, and it healed up. But where the hose had been, I ended up with what looked like an upside-down mountain. There were no antibiotics or other miracle drugs back then, so I was probably lucky to survive.

The first house that I can remember living in was in Fredonia, Kansas. I can remember very little about it. I was still too young to be in school. It was a small, one-story house. What I recall best about that house is that we had trouble paying the rent, and we'd hide under the bed when the landlord came knocking on the front door to collect the rent. That's about all. There were a lot of people during those days who were in the same boat.

After that, we lived in Coyville, Kansas. Every place I lived as a child was down in the southeast corner of Kansas. The first home of which I really have any memory was in Coyville. My dad had his barbershop in the house. We had no electricity, so he used hand clippers that he'd squeeze to cut hair. It was probably the same pair of clippers that he had used during World War I, when he was cutting hair for the troops in the trenches in France.

The house in Coyville wasn't big. There was no central heat. We just had a stove in the living room. It burned coal. You shoveled coal in, and you shoveled the cinders out. In the kitchen, there was an icebox, into which you put ice for cooling. The house had a screened-in back porch. Mom would set a bowl of milk out on the porch, and the cream would rise on it.

In addition to the house, we had a barn. And we had one cow. I was too little to remember much else. I was still riding a tricycle.

The first house that I have a better memory of was probably back in Fredonia, Kansas. We moved there again when I was about ten years old. It was around 1941. The house we lived in there had a living room, a kitchen, one or two bedrooms, and maybe a bathroom. Some of our houses didn't have bathrooms.

We always had some kind of a garden. You had to have one, if you wanted to eat.

I had a little red wagon. I can remember walking with Dad along the railroad tracks, pulling my little wagon and picking up coal that fell off of railroad cars to heat our house. Dad would put it in my wagon to take home. We just grew up with shortages, but everybody was in the same boat. We thought it was just the way of life. Today's inconveniences, due to the virus, are nothing compared with the inconveniences of those days.

We also took my little red wagon when we went down to the welfare office to get groceries. I can't recall the name of it. We got a lot of homily and grapefruit, and things of that nature.

Then, when I was ten or eleven, the Japanese attacked Pearl Harbor. Nothing really changed. There were wage and rent freezes. The common people didn't have a lot of money during World War II. But everybody was in the same boat. But then, there was even less to buy. In my mind, the Great Depression really didn't end until after the war. Until then, there was rationing, and there were price controls and food shortages.

We had a radio. It looked rather like a chest of drawers. It was a floor model. I tell my kids, we used to have a fishbowl sitting on top. We'd watch the fish swim while listening to the radio, and that was our TV.

On Saturdays, I would go to a movie with at least one of my sisters. I remember that, at one time, the admission to the movie was a couple of rat tails. Yes, real rat tails! Another time, it was a can of grease. They used it in the making of nitroglycerin.

From time to time, we had a car. Dad wrecked one of them. I think that was while we were living in Fredonia. His story was that there were barriers along the side of the road that were there to keep you from going into the ditch. He was trying the car out, and in the process hit the barrier, and wrecked the car. I'm sure that is not exactly how it happened. Then, for a long time, we didn't have a car. During the war, we had a '32 Chevy Coupe with a rumble seat. I learned to drive in that car. But most of the time, we didn't have a car.

I began school while we were living in Coyville. There was a one room schoolhouse, with one teacher. If I can recall, all the grades were together. We got to school in those days on foot, but Coyville was a small town. It wasn't a long walk—perhaps six blocks or so. I can't recall for sure.

Prior to World War II, my mother worked, at times, outside the home. She worked for a while at a poultry place, where they raised chickens. And she worked for a laundry, where she ironed sheets on a big Mandral sheet-ironing machine. That was a hot job. Those were the days before air-conditioning.

On Sundays, Dad liked to go fishing. He always wore a white shirt and a bow tie, even when he went fishing. We'd walk along the railroad tracks to the river, then across the trestle to get down to the river to fish. That was when we lived in Fredonia. We fished on the Verdigris River.

One day, my dad and I went fishing at the creek near our house in Coyville. We found a baby chicken wandering around. There had been gypsies camped there the night before, and we assumed that they had accidentally left it behind. We took it home, and l pulled it around in a trailer that my dad had made for my tricycle. The trailer was made from an orange crate. Back then, oranges were shipped to grocery stores in wooden crates. The grocery stores would give the crates to anyone who wanted them. We made all kinds of things from the wood of orange crates. My tricycle trailer was about twelve inches wide. At first, my little chicken would ride very comfortably inside. I named him Oswald. But then as Oswald grew older, he started standing on the top of the crate with one foot on each side. Now, twelve inches was quite a distance for a half-grown chicken to span with its two feet. When old Oswald grew up, I had the only bow-legged chicken in the neighborhood.

And there's one last story comes to mind. One winter, a fellow offered to pay my dad ten cents for each rabbit that he could shoot and dress out. Dad came home with a bunch of rabbits, but the guy reneged on his offer. We ate a lot of rabbit for the rest of the winter!

CHAPTER 8

IN THOSE DAYS, THE FIREMEN WOULD TAKE IN OLD, DISCARDED TOYS—OLD BICYCLES AND SLEDS. THEY WOULD FIX THEM UP AND MAKE THEM USABLE. THEY REPAIRED THEM AND PAINTED THEM AND MADE THEM LIKE NEW. THEY WOULD THEN BE GIVEN TO CHILDREN AS PRESENTS AT CHRISTMASTIME.

- MARILYN HANNON -
(Born January 12, 1926. Died November 4, 2020.)

I was born on January 12, 1926. I'm ninety-four right now. My mother was born in Maywood, Illinois. My dad had no relatives that we knew of. None. He was an only child and both of his parents were gone.

My mother's mother had a rooming house, a block away from us. Around 1908, my grandmother and other women were instrumental in getting a Catholic church, St. James, built in Maywood. My grandmother had come from Ireland, and although Catholic, she and my grandfather had been married in the Episcopal church.

There were seven in my family. I had two sisters and two brothers. My sister, Naomi, who was born in 1919, just passed away last September. She would have been one hundred years-old in November of 2019. (She was named after my dad's mother.) My brother, Eugene, was the second oldest. He was born in 1921. Then there was George, who was born in 1924. He became a Chicago fireman and retired as a battalion chief. He followed in his father's footsteps. I was the fourth oldest. I was born in 1926. My younger sister, Delores, was born in 1930. I'm the only one who is still alive.

The American Can Company came into Maywood before I was born, and it became a very big deal. It was a huge factory. All the kids used to work there, at some time or other. There were railroad cars, and the boys would pack the box cars that ran onto the sidings with boxes of cans. It employed a lot of people. Maywood was a very nice town in those days.

Before the American Can Company came to Maywood, Maywood had had a volunteer fire department. After American Can moved in, it was converted into a full-time fire department.

My father had been a volunteer fireman. But from the time I was born, I can always remember dad being "the chief." My dad was the fire chief in Maywood, Illinois through all my growing-up years.

There were two fire stations in town. One was in the south end of town; the other was right near us, on 5th Avenue at St. Charles Road. We only lived a couple blocks from the 5th Avenue station. We spent a lot of time there. They had two fire engines at that station. One was a ladder truck, and the other was a pumper. The pumper carried water. They were big fire trucks. I actually have a book about the Maywood Fire Department.

During the Depression, the firemen got paid only half salary, but they were given tax credits or certificates by the village to pay the taxes on their homes. This was so they didn't lose their homes. As kids, we knew that. Mom had probably told us.

In those days, the firemen would take in old, discarded toys—old bicycles and sleds. They would fix them up and make them usable. They repaired them and painted them and made them like new. They would then be given to children as presents at Christmastime.

The firemen also did another good thing. They put together food baskets. My two older brothers would then help deliver them to poor families. There were a lot of families that didn't have a dad, or where the dad didn't have a job. My brothers always made sure that our friends, who were poor, got two! The baskets were given around Thanksgiving and Christmas.

During the 1930s, I went to grade school at St. James. The school was part of the church building. The church was on the first floor, the classrooms were on the second, and the nuns lived in empty classrooms on the third floor. The pastor, Fr. James O'Shea*, had arrived from Ireland, and enjoyed living in a comfortable rectory. As fire chief of Maywood, my father told our pastor that if a fire broke out, and if anything happened to the nuns in the third-floor classrooms, there would be trouble. Eventually, the church paid to have a slide placed on the side of the building so that in case of fire, the nuns could escape. The nuns were eventually housed in a nice convent across the street. In case of fire, the students' only way of escape was by way of the stairs. But my father saw to it that fire drills were conducted every month. Similar drills were conducted in all of the schools in Maywood.

As a young girl, when I was in high school, I worked in the Woolworth's Dime Store after school. I worked there with two girlfriends. We normally worked two hours after school. But on Thursdays, the store was open until 9 p.m. So, we worked four hours on Thursdays, and then all day on Saturdays. We were paid twenty-nine cents per hour!

The store was just a big dime store. We'd work in the candy section. We'd weigh the candy and put it in a bag. Of course, we worked wherever we were needed, and we also did a lot of the office work. We'd check the inventory—what they needed and what they didn't need. The three of us worked there for three years, and then we all quit at the same time, because we were graduating from high school. I can recall that they were somewhat upset with us, because some of the ladies who worked there couldn't do the office-type work that we could do. They could sell things, but they couldn't do the paperwork and the checking to see what should be ordered, like we could. We did a lot of that.

As I have said, I had two brothers and a sister who were older than I was. On Saturday nights, they would sell the Sunday morning paper in front of the Lido Theater in Maywood. In those days, the Lido was a very popular theater. Everybody went to the show. The police used to bring my brothers home after the last show was over, late Saturday night, around midnight. My brothers made two cents for each paper they sold. I can't remember the price of the paper in those days; probably a dime.

Then on Sunday mornings, the guys in the paper delivery trucks would throw the papers on our front porch. They'd deliver them in sections. The papers weren't "stuffed." They were in sections. And we used to get up really early and "stuff" the papers. We'd insert all the different sections to get them ready to go. I can remember, as a little girl, stuffing them on our living room rug. There'd be at least a hundred or so papers when we got done. The firemen had made my brothers a big cart. My brothers would carry the papers in that cart. Underneath, it had big doors where they could load the papers. It was closed in, but it had an opening in the front. They would put the papers in the cart, and then push the cart about a block over to our church, St. James Catholic Church. And when Mass was out, people would buy the papers.

During the Depression, my mother did not work outside our home. Few mothers did. I don't recall one mother that worked outside the home.

We had a big two-story house. It was a very nice house. It had four bedrooms and a sun parlor. My uncle was a carpenter, and my mom had had him add on two big rooms—one upstairs and the other downstairs. It was a big house, and it's still there. The five of us kids occupied two of the bedrooms. The girls were in one room, and the boys were in another. We had a roomer. He lived in our home all the while I was there. He was an Irish guy, Walter Drinnen. He was single, and he was a mechanic. When he couldn't pay the rent, he'd paint a room, or paint the house, or fix something. He didn't eat with us ever. And I remember that he wouldn't give his rent money to my dad; he had to pay my mom. Three bucks a week or something. He had been raised by a lady, and my mom would talk to her from time-to-time on the phone and let her know how he was doing. He died at Hines Hospital when I was eighteen years old. By that time, I had just started nursing school.

Our house had plumbing, and we had electricity. We always had electricity. We also had central heating. They put the central heat in when I was just learning to walk. It would have been in 1927. That was pretty early! It used ten tons of coal a year! We never had a "stoker." We had my brothers and my father to shovel. They were the stokers!

We had a hot water heater, also. You had to light it, and then you had to remember to shut it off. We didn't have an icebox. We never bought ice from the iceman, although most of the people on the block did. My mom or one of us kids would go to the store every day, and we'd carry home the butter and milk. We never had an icebox, but very early, somewhere along the line, my dad picked up a Kelvinator refrigerator. So, we had ice cubes. It was wonderful. It was a big deal. We'd make little frozen popsicles.

We also had a big radio. It was one of those that sat on the floor. I can't remember the make. It was one where you could tune in and get broadcasts from overseas. I can remember Dad, when I was a little kid, showing us how to get overseas broadcasts on the shortwave band. Our radio was a big deal. We listened to everything on the radio. We used to sit and listen. My dad loved to listen to the church music—the Negro spirituals—that were broadcast on Chicago radio on Sunday nights. But mostly, we listened to the ball games—Bob Elson and the White Sox. My father was a big White Sox fan. I didn't like sports until I got married. (Then I had to like them! Or I shouldn't have gotten married! My husband was from the south side of Chicago, and he was a huge White Sox fan.)

And we went to the movies. We had passes because my dad was fire chief. My girlfriend and I used to love the Nelson Eddy and Jeanette MacDonald movies, and the Shirley Temple movies. My girlfriend, Gwen, lived next door. We went to the movies together. We were the same age. We were only four days apart and we were inseparable. She just died a few years ago. Her mom died when she was a little girl, so my mom kind of covered for hers.

As kids, we played jump rope, a lot of *Monopoly*, and we played baseball with the boys in the vacant lot behind us.

My mom had a garden. She grew tomatoes and rhubarb. Well, rhubarb would actually grow wild. And we had cherry trees. All the stuff that we didn't eat got canned. My mom wasn't a huge canner, but she did can the cherries. We were a large family, so we ate the rest. We didn't waste food. We ate a lot of rhubarb, and it was good with a lot of sugar. I loved it.

My mother had a sewing machine, and she sewed. It was a White Electric sewing machine. There was a thing she pushed with her knee to the side to make it go.

My father always bragged that we always had milk and butter. We were kids that didn't go without that type of thing. With the five kids and my mom, we used a gallon of milk a day. We took turns going to pick up the milk. There was a dairy at 1st Avenue and Lake Street. We'd take our jug and cut through the park to get there. There was a huge park—five blocks along the railroad tracks—and we would get the milk at twenty-one cents per gallon. They would fill the jug up.

We were in the park all the time. But we had to cross a busy street to get there. There was a playground there, with a little merry-go-round that you sat on, and little swings and slides. And they had an ice skating rink. Kids could ice skate there.

And there were holiday parades. We belonged to the American Legion. This was after World War I. My mother was with the Legion Auxiliary. I belonged to the Junior Legion.

Men would come to the house and ask for food. The railroad came through our town, and the men would get off. They would live along 1st Avenue, along the Des Plaines River, by the forest preserve along the eastern edge of Maywood. Some of them would hang out in tents set up behind Proviso East High School. They would come around and ask or beg for food. My mom always fed them in back of the house, on the steps. We had the kitchen and a breakfast room, and she'd feed them.

One time, I was helping my mom, although she generally did not take much help from us kids. She generally preferred to do things herself. She was very efficient. But that day, I was helping her hang clothes in the back yard, and a hobo came around the back, and when she looked up, she realized that she knew him. And he knew her. They had gone to high school together. It was very embarrassing for both of them. It was sort of a sad meeting. I was old enough to realize that they were both very embarrassed.

And I can remember men coming to the door, selling thread. It was always thread. It was ten cents for a spool of thread. My mom bought a lot of thread. She always had a dime to buy thread.

And then, there was a man with a pony. He went down the street taking pictures of children. The man would put a child on the pony. He would then take the child's picture and expect the child's parents to pay for the picture. My mother would have killed us if we had let him trick us into sitting on his pony so he could take our pictures. She had no desire to be dunned for photos that she had not permitted to be taken.

And there was also the "ding-dong man." He pushed a cart and he would sharpen scissors and knives. He rang a bell as he went down the street, so we called him the ding-dong man. And there was the iceman. And we had "Pete the Peddler." He came with vegetables on his truck, and he'd stop in the middle of the block, and sell fresh vegetables to the women along the block. He had a truck, not a horse. But I seem to remember horses delivering milk. But we never bought milk from the milkman. We got our milk at the dairy, where there was a little store. And there was the "rags, old iron man" who came down the alley. My brothers dealt with him, but they never trusted him. He used to weigh the papers, but my brothers were a step ahead of him. You got money for your newspapers.

Then, we had the WPA. That was a big deal in our town. The WPA put in our storm sewers. My mother loved it because we never had a flooded basement. I don't know if our basement flooded before that, but I know my mother was very happy. They put them in between the sidewalk and the curb. They dug in the parkway. They were working there for years. I think they did the whole darn town.

And I can recall when our neighbors—our friends—got scarlet fever. They put a sign out so no one could go in that house. It was a quarantine sign. It was like putting out the sign for the iceman, only it was an orange quarantine sign. That was the only quarantine sign I can ever recall seeing.

In those days, the doctors made house calls. They made them all the way up through World War II. Our family doctor was our pediatrician, and he was very prominent. His name was Dr. William Raycraft. He lived and practiced in River Forest, adjacent to Maywood. He made house calls, as did all doctors at the time. He made them mostly in the evenings, after office hours.

When I was in eighth grade or a freshman in high school, I sometimes took care of the doctor's children while he worked. His wife had passed away and had left him with four children. He had a housekeeper, but I would watch his kids during the day in the summertime. I was over there a lot. I babysat and took care of his children. And I also took care of the children of a lot of other families. I was very involved in taking care of their children. Sometimes, the doctor would say, "Let's go for a ride," and the kids and I would go with him when he made his house calls. While he worked, we'd be out in the yard.

There was a man who lived down the street from Dr. Raycraft named Lawrence Welk. You know who Lawrence Welk was! Dr. Raycraft also took care of Lawrence Welk's children. Later, when I became a nurse, I'd fill in for Dr. Raycraft's nurse when she was on vacation or otherwise couldn't be at work. I had known Mr. Welk earlier, but when I filled in as a nurse, I gave his kids their shots.

When my sister, Naomi, went to nursing school, Dr. Raycraft was one of her teachers. When she completed nursing school, she went to work for him. Then she joined the army, because many nurses were needed in the army. She was in the South Pacific during the war. She was in New Guinea, and later she was in the Philippine invasion. Both of my brothers were also in the service. My one brother was in Europe during the war, and my other, who was involved with the air corps, stayed in this country. All three were gone, and I was in nursing school. At the time, we had very few nurses at the nursing school, only the nuns. The nursing students did most of the work. We were too young to realize how scary it was.

At this point, all my siblings and friends are gone. I'm the only one left. But I've found a new home and new friends in my assisted living residence.

* Father James O'Shea and the author are unrelated, to the best of my knowledge.

CHAPTER 9

WE HAD DAD'S WAKE RIGHT IN THE HOUSE. WE COULDN'T SPARE THE MONEY FOR A FUNERAL PARLOR. SO, WE HAD THE CASKET RIGHT IN THE HOUSE.

- DAN HOHMEIER -
(Born December 24, 1926)

I was born on Christmas Eve, December 24, 1926. I'm ninety-three. There were eight in my family: my father, my mother, four brothers, a sister, and myself.

Our home was on Fairfield Avenue, just south of Devon Avenue, on the north side of Chicago. The address was 6331 N. Fairfield. It was somewhat of a Jewish neighborhood. Our house was a pretty nice two-story house. My parents must have had a pretty good mortgage on it, but they never told us.

There were four bedrooms. Two boys shared one bedroom, three boys had a second bedroom (we could slide another bed in it), and our sister had her own bedroom. That worked out quite well. We were very content with that set up. Of course, we didn't have a whole lot of stuff.

We did have electricity, but for "air-conditioning," we had a fan that we blew over a bowl of water, so we'd at least have the proper amount of humidity.

The house was heated with a furnace. It was a coal furnace. When we wanted coal, we'd call up my uncle. He was the guy who'd deliver the coal. We had a window in the basement, and he'd dump the coal through that window into the basement. There was kind of a room there, which we called the coal shed. That's where the coal went. Then, we'd go in there to get coal to put in the furnace. In the mornings, we'd have to get up to start the fire. That wasn't too bad. But it cut into our time. We could never do any school work in the morning because we had to get the fire going. And there was a "shaker" under the furnace, which allowed all the furnace ash to fall down into a little pit at the bottom. We would take all the ash out of the pit and spread it out in the alley. The alley was paved with all the discarded coal ashes. We never got gas heat in that house. Even when we finally sold the house, we still used coal.

My dad was a carpenter by trade. He worked for his brother. It was a pretty good job, but we were poor. It seemed like everybody was. We thought Dad made pretty good money at the time, but obviously, it was not all that good.

What I remember best of those days are hand-me-downs. I came from a family of four brothers and one sister. So, whenever they got too big for their clothes or they didn't want them anymore, they handed them down to me. "You can take these clothes now, and wear them, because I'm going to get some new junk tomorrow." I rarely got new clothes. We accepted that. We were poor. We didn't have the money, and we thought that was the best way to do it—to get the most use out of the clothes.

Of course, we had shoes. But we never really handed shoes down. When the soles wore down, we'd cut out a piece of cardboard, and put it in the front part of the shoe where you would normally wear a hole in the shoe. That worked fairly well. If the hole got to where it started to wear the sock out, we'd take two cardboard pieces and put them in. We kept doing that until it got too thick. We'd also buy flaps, which were shaped like the front part of the shoe. We'd glue them on. Unfortunately, the minute the shoe got a little damp, the glue would come loose, and you'd be walking down the street, with your sole flapping away. That was kind of embarrassing at school—to have a shoe with a flapping flap. But we didn't have the money for a new pair of shoes, and nobody was handing down any. So, we just had to make do. You'd glue on a flap, or put more cardboard in it.

We always had to buy bargains, or go to stores and buy what was left over. That's how we saved our money. The bargains were mostly on food. But then, when they had sales on clothes, we'd try to get them. Rarely did I ever get anything new. We had a Lublaw store in the neighborhood. I think Jewel came in and bought them out. We went over there whenever they had bargains.

Mom sewed. She was a very good sewer. She sewed up all our clothes to repair them. That's how we functioned, because she was able to repair them. And she darned. She darned lots of socks. I don't think they do that anymore. She stuck something right in the sock that would give kind of a solid backing for the needle and the thread as she sewed. I don't think she liked doing it, but she did it.

Mom was also our family disciplinarian. If we did something wrong, for a punishment, we had to go down in the basement and our mother would whack us with a stick across our butts. Depending on how bad our infraction was, she'd whack us a sufficient number of times to make us feel like we never wanted to do again what we had done.

But we got smart after a while. We'd find the weakest stick we could find down there. There were sticks in the basement because Dad was a carpenter. But then my mother got wise, too, and she'd say, "Bring me a real stick." Then we had to think real fast. So, we thought the best way to get her a stick that looked like a good stick was to saw it half-way through. We tried that, and that seemed to work pretty well. We'd rub the stick over with a little bit of glue and a little bit of saw dust, and it looked okay.

My mother had an unnatural craving for mulberries. As luck would have it, there was a mulberry tree next door, on the vacant lot. We'd climb up into the tree—somehow, we never fell out—and we'd get her a rather large bowl of mulberries. She really used to like those things. And she used to like for us to massage her head a lot. I don't know if that was punishment, or she just liked to have us do it. That and mulberries were her two favorite things.

In our family, around the house, everybody had a job to do. My sister did most of the cleaning, and some of the cooking. That was the bulk of the work. My mother was a little bit tough on her. During the week, my sister cooked the oatmeal for breakfast, and on Sundays she'd make cocoa, instead of just plain milk. Having cocoa to drink was a rather nice treat.

There were five brothers and one sister in our family. So naturally, we tried to push most of the stuff off onto our sister—all the cooking, ironing, and cleaning. She did all of that. Of course, she complained about it. But who could blame her?

When we would take a bath, two boys would bathe at the same time to conserve water. Our sister, of course, was never allowed to come in while we were bathing. But she'd complain that we wouldn't clean the ring around the tub. So, she had to do that, too, and she felt kind of put out.

I lived at the Fairfield address until I was about ten or twelve years old. Then we moved, because my dad died. He died early.

As I said, Dad was a carpenter. He worked for his brother, who owned the shop. He cut himself at his brother's shop. They tried to stop the bleeding too soon, and he caught a clot. He died at age forty-four. I was twelve when my father died.

We had Dad's wake right in the house. We couldn't spare the money for a funeral parlor. So, we had the casket right in the house. And people came in, and brought hams and everything else. We hadn't had so much food in a long time. But, of course, we fed some of the people who were there. The rest of the burial went pretty much the same way as burials do now, with the hearse going to the cemetery, and all that.

When Dad was alive, we didn't have a car. He could get the street car on Devon, right near where he worked, and it would drop him off, right at our corner, and he could walk straight over to our house. That was rather nice.

We did not get a car until quite sometime after Dad had died. We eventually got a second-hand car. It worked, but we didn't know how to work it that well. At first, we didn't realize that the brake was on, and when we tried to drive, we'd leave a trail of white smoke. That's how we found out it did have brakes, and we shouldn't be driving with the brake on!

Dad's death put a big dent in our income. It put us in a bind. We boys all had to go out and get paper routes. We each had a number of different paper routes. We survived on that. I delivered the *Daily News*. Did you ever hear of that? I had a bit of a hard time. My throw was always a bit off. You'd roll the paper up to throw it. I was a bit wild. Sometimes when I threw it, the paper would land up on the roof! Because I didn't have any extra ones, they just wouldn't get one that day—without climbing. Sometimes, they hollered at me a lot.

I also delivered the *Downtown Shopper*. Some guy, for some reason, hated that paper so much that he threatened to throw me off the porch. Well, that kind of scared me, at that age. But even with the paper routes, we couldn't afford much. We had the bare essentials. We had the same stuff we had previously, but just less of it. We were always working to bring money into the house. Everybody brought in whatever they could. Needless to say, we weren't a rich family. We weren't even middle class. In fact, we were rather poor.

Then when we got in high school, we had a little more freedom, and we got jobs that paid somewhat better. I worked in a grocery store, in the delicatessen department. Once, as I was opening the door to the refrigerated counter, where they stored all the meats—sausages, cheeses, and all that—there was another guy working there. He tended to be a bit careless. He slammed the counter door, and it caught my thumb. It really, really hurt and it started to swell up. I asked, "What am I going to do now?" And he said "Stick it up your [butt] and go home!" That was the extent of his consideration.

For enjoyment, we would play ball in that vacant lot next door to us. That's where we did all our baseball stuff. We played both softball and baseball. We'd pitch and hit softballs to see how far we could hit them. Fortunately, we did not break the windows in our house, which was right next door to the lot. And we played whatever other sports we wanted to play, including football. But we didn't play tackle football. That was a little too hard on our clothes.

We also used the lots on either side of our house for playing other games, like hide-and-go-seek. We'd punish the guys who were hiding. We'd just stand around for a while, and let the mosquitos eat them, until they came out of their hiding places. We played a lot of games, including marbles.

We had bicycles, which was somewhat surprising, given our limited amount of money. We all had bicycles. We paid two dollars apiece for them. That was our enjoyment. They were our main way of getting anywhere. We went pretty far with those things. To buy a new one was out of our price range.

We had radios in those days. That's all we had. About the only program that I can recall is *Fibber McGee and Molly*. We didn't listen to any kids' shows in the afternoon. We had to get our homework done. We had good grades. I wouldn't say we were smart, but we had a lot of homework to do. We had to do the homework before we could do anything else.

We went to the movies. I don't recall what they were, but we went. They were really nice entertainment. We didn't go on Saturdays; instead, we just worked around the house. One of our chores, when we were bad, was to pull weeds. I never pulled so many weeds in my life.

Oh, I just remembered. We had a washing machine when we lived on Fairfield. I don't remember the make of the machine, but it had a big capacity. We got the bright idea of giving each other rides. A person could fit inside if you didn't have clothes in it. And since it didn't have an agitator, we thought . . . but then, we thought that might be carrying things too far.

But while we never got rides in that old washing machine, one day my brother and I got a ride on it! It was on spin dry. We had put it on spin dry, and when we looked around, it was gone! So, we began searching for it, and there it was in a different part of the basement! It was chugging away. So, we—my younger brother and I—tried to stop it. He grabbed one side and I grabbed the other side, and it dragged us all around the basement, as far as the cord would allow. We didn't know where the switch was to shut it off. Finally, when it got near enough to where the plug was, we were able to get hold of the plug. We pulled the plug, and we were finally able to stop it. It was just full of water. We had a heck of a time dragging it to a level spot where it wouldn't travel around the room again.

When you opened the gate in our backyard fence, right across the alley was the entrance to St. Timothy's Catholic Church. We went to St. Timothy's. The school there went up through eighth grade. I went four years there. And then you went to high school. It was kind of nice; in fact, it was very nice. The nuns showed us a bit of special kindness. They would bring stuff over from time to time. They knew we were rather hard-up.

In those days, there were men who plied the streets and alleys of the city.

The iceman was one of them. When the iceman came around, he'd look at our window. He had given us a cardboard thing, a nice-looking thing. It had been made-up professionally. On its sides, it read 25, 50, 75 and 100. Well, we never were able to afford a hundred pounds at a time, so our maximum was seventy-five pounds. But even to buy that much was very rare. And we'd always go and get the scraps of ice that he had chipped away. We would suck on that.

And then there was the watermelon man. He came around selling watermelons. We'd ask, "How do we know if it is any good?" He'd say, "I'll cut it in half for you." We'd say, "No, no, no, you don't want to cut it in half." So, he'd do what was called "plugging." He'd take a knife and stick it in at three or four angles, and then pull the piece out. That was the "plug." We always waited for that plug. It seemed to me a good way to find out if a watermelon was good or not.

And there were also ragmen who came down the alley. "Rags, old iron." And we used to call them the "rags, old iron men." They'd take paper, too. But they wanted it bundled. We gave them bundled papers and rags. We didn't have much iron. Just a lot of rags. They used a truck.

There were very few horses, at the time, in our neighborhood. The rag-men came down the alleys a couple times a month.

We kept things going for a while, but finally it came to the point where we could no longer make full payments on the house. So, then we had to move into a flat. It was close to River View Park, near Roscoe. It was all right. The neighborhood was nice. One thing . . . we never, never had neighborhood trouble. Everybody tried to take care of themselves, and wouldn't try to fight with anybody else. We didn't have anything like we have now. It's ridiculous! As a kid during the Depression, you didn't know what was out there. Whether it was something better or something worse. So, we just went with the flow.

CHAPTER 10

ONE SUNDAY, MOTHER DECIDED TO TAKE US FOR A WALK. WE WALKED UP THIS HILL INTO A WOODED AREA. WHAT WE CAME UPON, I LATER LEARNED, WAS A BOOTLEG STILL.

- DAWN BARTEL -
(Born January 16, 1925)

Dad had gone to Ames College in Iowa, and Mom had gone to Coe College in Cedar Rapids, Iowa. At that time, when they were in college, Ames was definitely an agricultural college. So, my dad's joke was, "Mother went to Coe College and I went to Cow College." They both were very concerned that their children would get good educations. They were very determined in that.

Well, my father and mother bought a farm about the time they got married. It was down in Missouri, right across from the Illinois side. Dad raised cane, which he took to have processed into molasses. He raised watermelons. My dad never would raise cotton. Then they lost that farm. After that, my dad became what he called a "tenant farmer," which actually was a sharecropper. Life was hard. Very hard, because they both came from large, fairly well-off families.

My brother was born about two years before I was. I was born on a farm near Wapello, Iowa on January 16, 1925. It was an at-home birth. We lived on that farm just outside of Wapello until I was a little over three years old. I don't remember much about that farm itself. It was a little way from town, and I seem to recall that there was a long driveway from the house out to the main road. It probably wasn't that long, but to a two-and-a-half or three-year-old, it seemed a long way. I have no memory of my parents ever taking us into Wapello, or anything like that.

Our home there was an old farmhouse. I can remember that when we lived there, my dad lifted up the linoleum covering the kitchen floor, and there was a door in the floor. He opened it up. Later, he and my mother told me that the house had been an Underground Railroad station during the Civil War. Slaves heading north could hide there. That trapdoor in the kitchen led down to a low cellar. They told us that they didn't want us around the trapdoor. I never did go down to take a peek; I was too young. I don't know whether my folks ever did. All that I can really remember is that someone had put down linoleum to cover the old trapdoor.

We lived there outside of Wapello until I was three and a half. Then we moved to Sikeston, Missouri. Sikeston is down in the boot of Missouri, as I recall. We lived there probably a year.

I had my fourth birthday in Sikeston. It was special. I remember it because it was the first time that I can recall candles on the cake. I tried to blow them out, but I didn't do too well. I wasn't allowed to get too near them.

Our house in Sikeston was pretty simple. The kitchen, of course, had a cook stove. And there was a counter on which there was a pail of water. There was a common dipper for the water. No wonder people died! They passed things on to each other! And there was also a room that we called the living room.

The house in Sikeston also had a couple of bedrooms, in addition to the living room and kitchen. There was a stove in the living room. When we could afford it, we'd use coal. If not, we burned wood that was available from trees and branches on the farm. But usually, we'd get a load of coal. Dad would stoke the stove before going to bed at night, and there would still be embers inside to start a fire again in the morning. And of course, in the kitchen there was a big, old cast-iron stove. The two stoves threw off a good amount of heat. But there wasn't any heat in the bedrooms, except what came from the stove in the living room. But we had quilts in the bedrooms.

One thing that I can recall is that every time we moved, my mother and dad bought wall-covering and papered the walls in the house that we were moving into. My mother was always a very neat housekeeper. She was very fussy about how things looked. She was a very particular woman. For years, and all through the Depression, she was very private and didn't make very many friends, because she couldn't afford to entertain them. The married life that she was living was a very different life from the one she had led as a young person, when she had more advantages. But she and my dad made life nice for us kids.

I can recall going into Sikeston with my parents and going into the grocery store. We lived in Sikeston for a year or two, and then we moved to Perkins, Missouri. That's where my brother started school. He was six and I was four when we moved to Perkins.

In Perkins we lived in a two-story house. I had an upstairs bedroom, and there was a metal grate in the floor. It was just a hole in the floor, so I was warned never to mess with the grate, because it could be lifted up. It was just above the living room. The heat rose through it and heated the bedroom a bit.

In that house, we had two wood stoves for heating. One was in the living room, in the main part of the house. Then there was a big, old cast iron stove in the kitchen, with a water tank on one side. So, if you had a fire in the stove, you always had warm water. We had no indoor plumbing. We had outhouses. We had a pump in the yard.

We had an interesting experience in Perkins. There were hills nearby. On Sundays, Mom and Dad would take us for a stroll. Besides looking at the flowers and trees, we'd explore a bit. One Sunday, Mother decided to take us for a walk. We walked up this hill into a wooded area. What we discovered there, I later learned, was a bootleg still. Fortunately, there wasn't anyone around. Nevertheless, my mother quickly turned us around and took us home. She warned us never to talk about it. She said it was something that was there that shouldn't have been there, and that we shouldn't talk about it. So, we didn't—until we moved again. Then I asked her about it. She said it was an illegal still. "Who knows what would have happened if we had spread the word?"

We stayed in Perkins just a year. I moved a lot as a kid. We kept moving, because that's what tenant farmers did. Things were pretty bad in those days. No one had a lot. But we didn't need a lot. We got along fine, but it was hard on my parents. They both had come from families that had a little bit more, and had nice homes.

Next, we moved to Malden, Missouri. We lived around Malden probably the longest. When we went to Malden, we lived on a farm for a year or two.

Then we moved into town. Because my dad had a tractor, the cotton mill in town hired him. It was a relief from farm work. He had regular hours, and we had a little house in Malden.

When Dad went to work at the mill, my brother and I began to get allowances—twelve cents a week! The two cents, we always spent on candy. There was a place in town where we could get a lot of candy for two cents. They would have leftover Christmas candy that had all melted together—they didn't have refrigeration. For a penny or two, you could get several pieces of candy. So, we thought that we were pretty well off.

The remaining dime we spent going to the movies every Saturday afternoon. In those days, there were serials. At the end of every episode, the hero always ended up being tied to the railroad tracks! So, we had to go back the next Saturday to find out how he saved himself. I can't remember the names of any of the serials, but they were wonderful, and kept us spending our dimes every week.

I started school when we lived in Malden. I went to a couple of country schools. My brother was already in school. As I have said, he was two years older than I was.

But the teacher and I didn't get along. I think I was a little bit rebellious. I got spanked pretty often. That first year—well it wasn't a complete year—I didn't really learn anything.

Then one day, out in the school yard, a kid got mad at me for some reason. I don't think I was a very nice child. He threw a board at me with a nail in it. And I got quite a nasty scratch on my leg. I went in, and the teacher said, "Wash it off and stop crying." That was about the extent of her interest in me. But she loved my brother.

When I got home, Mother looked at it and said, "Didn't they put anything on it?" I said, "My teacher doesn't like me." Mother and Dad became concerned. Until then, they had been kind of ignoring my progress, perhaps because things weren't going all that well, and perhaps because Mother was expecting another baby. But Dad got pretty irritated.

There was another school about equidistant from our house. Dad enrolled us there. The teacher was a man. His name was Dan Tyler. He was the kindest, and most sympathetic teacher, and the most wonderful mentor. He became very good friends with our family. He and my dad talked together a lot. He told my folks, "That boy is really smart . . . he's really, really smart, but I don't know about that girl"—meaning me! But within a year or two I had learned to read, and he changed his opinion about me. He was a wonderful teacher.

And while we were living in Malden, I had another wonderful teacher. She was very sweet and kind. She liked me, and I was a good student. She wanted to put me a grade ahead. When you went to a country school, you listened to all the classes recite. You couldn't help hearing, because everybody was in one room. I was in third grade, but I did know some of the fourth-grade stuff. She wanted to move me up into fourth grade. She talked to my folks. My dad said that he "would like her to talk to Dan Tyler about it." But Dan thought, "No." He didn't think she ought to do it. He said, "Giver her a chance to be a kid." So, she didn't promote me.

Then the next year, the cotton plant burned down under very suspicious circumstances. The owner was found in the ruins, shot, and not by his own hand. No weapon was ever found. My dad's tractor had been moved out to a safe place, and my dad had been sent on an errand that day, and therefore wasn't in the building. It was all very mysterious and hush-hush.

My dad took his tractor and went back to another farm in the area. And we were back in school with Dan Tyler. So, I spent my fourth grade in a country school.

Then while I was in fifth grade in school, my dad decided to give up on farming. Dad decided that farming wasn't going to do it, so he began selling. At first, he sold straw hats.

We then moved to Cambridge, Illinois. And that was the first time that we lived in a house that had running water and indoor plumbing.

When we moved to Cambridge, Illinois, there was a library there. But we could only take three books out at a time. It was open only on Tuesdays, Fridays, and Saturdays. Three days a week. Every Saturday, I always cleaned up and went to the library. That was my big treat for Saturday. I'd get three books, and by Tuesday, I'd take those books back and get three more. I always got my maximum. The librarian was very strict about what would be age-appropriate. They had a whole shelf of Louisa May Alcott books, and boy, did I go through those. They were pretty exciting!

My dad had an Overland automobile. I don't think Overlands were in production very long. I don't know who made them. I think he eventually sold it. You had to have gas, and I don't think we could afford both gas and groceries. We preferred groceries. That car sat in the yard at a couple of the places where we lived. We didn't ride in it.

Instead, when Dad would go to town to buy groceries, he'd ride our horse, and take a gunnysack to carry the groceries. Sometimes, he'd hitch up the wagon and we'd all go in. That was always an adventure. And sometimes, if there was gas, we'd ride in the car. But it depended on what was available and how our finances were. Getting food was our main purpose for going into town. But we bought only the basics— flour, sugar. We pretty much raised the other things we needed. We grew our own vegetables, and of course, we had meat. We raised watermelons and peanuts. And we had cane for the molasses. It was a simple life, and I think a very hard one for my parents, because as I said, they both came from families that had more. But it was good for all of us in a way. We learned a lot of lessons. We learned how to make ourselves comfortable and happy with what we had.

During the Depression years, our food was very simple. We ate a lot of greens. Mother and Dad were both health conscious, and greens were cheap. We ate dandelion greens. One of my favorite dishes was scrambled eggs with greens. It sounds weird, and it was ugly. The greens added an ugly touch to the scrambled eggs. But I thought it was pretty flavorful. We used sorghum molasses for a lot of our sweetening. Mother made bread and biscuits. A loaf of white bread was a real treat. We didn't buy a lot of food at the grocery store, like they do nowadays. The meat we ate—we lived on farms—was butchered. My dad always said, "We never missed a meal." But there were a lot of meals that weren't very special.

I think I was in fifth grade before we got a radio. Some of our neighbors had radios, and I can remember listening to the report of the Lindbergh kidnapping on a neighbor's radio one evening while I was playing with their children. No, we didn't have a radio for quite a while.

Christmastime was always a treat. Mother and Dad always got a couple of coconuts, and we would crack them open, and pick out the coconut meat. Then we'd drink the coconut milk. That was really special.

Mom and Dad both liked to read. They encouraged us to read. We always had bedtime stories and goodnight hugs and kisses. Mother loved to make up stories, and we liked to have her make them up. She would tell us about a little boy and girl, Bob and Betty. They would have adventures. Mother would make up these adventures. And they read us all the Brothers Grimm fairy tale stories: "Little Red Riding Hood," "Goldilocks and the Three Bears," "Rapunzel," and all those stories. We always had a bedtime story. Sometimes they came from her imagination; other times they came from Grimms' Fairy Tales.

We did a lot of reading. My folks had books. I think one of the best Christmases, although my parents couldn't afford much, was when we were living near Malden, Missouri. Mother and Dad gave me the book *Little Women* by Louisa May Alcott, and they gave my brother the book *Little Men*, also by Louisa May Alcott. And, oh my goodness! I think we had those books read by the next morning. They were fascinating. Then we exchanged, so we could read each other's book.

Our games were simple. We played in the yard. You didn't worry about being outside without supervision. I learned to swim in a drainage canal. We were allowed to go explore.

There didn't seem to be the dangers. Or maybe people were just more trusting. Everything was pretty simple. We played tag, crack the whip, and at recess, we had swings and slides in the yard at school, and things that are probably outlawed now, because kids get hurt.

I stayed overnight with friends. We'd have boiled beans and greens for supper. And we'd sleep on the floor, but it was fun. That was our life.

We had stray dogs and cats. They were kept outside. People didn't have dogs inside like they do now. Although our cat pretty much stayed inside.

It was hard. It really was. Things were tough, but I think those of us who lived through the Depression learned to make do, to do over, and to do without. My mother repurposed everything. In those days, a lot of the things you bought in bulk came in cloth bags. I can remember her making aprons, tea towels, and things like that from cloth bags. I don't remember exactly what came in the bags, but I remember the bags. And being poor didn't hurt us. The Depression taught us all a lot of lessons. It made us stronger.

In some ways it was a very simple time because nobody had a lot. What made it bearable was that if you went without, you knew your friends were also going without.

Oh! I have one more little story! In later years, when my husband and I began to travel, I didn't have a birth certificate. So, I went to the courthouse at Wapello to get one, and the lady there—the clerk—asked me about my birth. She asked, "Do you know who the doctor was?" I told her the doctor's name, and she laughed. She said, "Oh, he was terrible about registering births! But if you say you were born, you probably were." Since I was, she gave me a birth certificate.

CHAPTER 11

THE GALBRAITH ADMINISTRATION DID AN AWFUL LOT TO SEPARATE THE STORM SEWERS FROM THE SANITARY SEWERS. . . . ROCK ISLAND ALSO BUILT ITS SEWAGE DISPOSAL PLANT [AND] ITS CENTRAL FIRE STATION. . . . ALL THESE IMPROVEMENTS WERE DONE WITH THE ASSISTANCE OF THE ROOSEVELT ADMINISTRATION.

- ARDO HOLMGRAIN -

I'm ninety-one now. I was born in 1928, about eighteen months before the stock market fell. I was about a year-and-a-half old when the stock market crashed.

My parents were conservative Republicans. In the late thirties, during the six years of the Galbraith administration, my dad was a Rock Island city councilman. The Galbraith administration did an awful lot to separate the storm sewers from the sanitary sewers. I believe that by the end of the Depression, Rock Island had completed the separation of its stormwater sewers from its sanitary sewers. And Rock Island also built its sewage disposal plant. That was the first time the city ever had proper sewage disposal. During those years, Rock Island also built its central fire station and got its large hook-and-ladder fire engine.

All these improvements were done with the assistance of the Roosevelt administration. It made the financing possible. During those years, the Civilian Conservation Corps (CCC) did outstanding things in Rock Island's Black Hawk Park.

The CCC built the stone inn—the Lodge—that is still in use today. They also built the smaller building that now houses the Hauberg Indian Museum, as well as a shelter down at the southeast end of the park. And they created many paths, bridges, and other improvements in the park. All this was done as a part of the CCC program.

During the Depression, Rock Island also built the Rock Island Reservoir, with the big domes covering it, at about 18th Avenue and 23rd Street in Rock Island. That domed reservoir system was built in a very nice neighborhood, and it created a lot of controversy. The residents, who had been looking into a nice green park area up until then, objected to the raised ground and the tanks that were being constructed. In the end, it was a great municipal improvement, but it came at the high cost of sacrificing residential park lands.

And I guess, I should mention the Centennial Bridge. That was a big deal. It was built in 1938 to span the Mississippi River between Rock Island and Davenport. When it was finished, the mothers, who were a YWCA group, got the kids together in Indian costumes, and the kids carried a banner about the YWCA and marched across the new bridge from Davenport to Rock Island. They were followed by car after car, and band after band. It was a big parade.

As a family, as I was growing up, we always had a vegetable garden. I think that was a common thing. We raised some corn in our garden, but it was not a favorite. A corn stalk is a pretty big plant, but out of that, you would only get one or maybe two ears of corn. We favored tomatoes and green beans. There were a lot of tomatoes. Mother would can tomatoes for the winter. And we also had leaf lettuce. For vegetables, that was about it. We also had a flower garden.

We never had guns, and we did no hunting, but I think it was a common thing to hunt. I think a lot of people hunted just to eat.

We did, however, fish. Our favorite spot was out by the old dam on the Rock River. Today, it's under the new bridge. Another good fishing spot along the Rock was just on the other side of the river, by the outlet for the old power house. We generally fished along the Rock River, not in the Mississippi. We would catch catfish, perch, and carp. I don't know that we ever got a game fish in that area. Although we fished for food, we also fished for entertainment.

In those years, my dad had a car. My father was a realtor. He sold farms. During the Depression, that was a very difficult business. If anything was sold, it was almost given away. Houses were like $2,500. There just wasn't any money.

There were five in our family. I was the youngest of three brothers. We each came five-and-a-half years apart. As soon as one of the kids was ready to start school, my mom and dad would have another kid. We lived in a house in the 800 block of 19th Street in Rock Island. Our home had the modern conveniences. We had running water, a bathroom, and three bedrooms. We lived two houses from the Cleaveland House.

The Cleaveland House was originally built by Dr. Stewart. His son bought or built a house right next to them. We were next door to the younger Stewart. It was a very diverse neighborhood. The average-income person lived there right along with the rich folks in those days.

By the way, the Whites and Cleavelands lived together there. Dorothy White was a Cleaveland. Actually, three generations of Cleavelands and Whites lived together there. I can recall the neighborhood children riding their scooters and trikes around and around the circular drive on the south side of the Cleaveland House. David and Marion White had wonderful toys to share during those Depression years. They had a huge train set in the basement.

After Sunday services at the nearby Broadway Presbyterian Church, Ted and Dorothy White would lead the neighbor kids across the new Centennial Bridge, which had been built in 1938, and return via the Government Bridge. Then, Ted would prepare a pancake brunch for the kids, seated at their big kitchen table.

Our neighbor across the street was June Haver. She was a beautiful blonde who was younger than I was. She became a famous Hollywood actress, and married the famous Hollywood actor Fred MacMurray. In October 1946, she traveled by train to Rock Island to attend the premier of *Three Little Girls in Blue* at the Fort Theatre.

We were very close to the kids in the neighborhood. We'd go around the neighborhood and holler for the kids to come out so we could get a ball game going. We had a telephone all my life, but we kids would just go out and holler for each other. We'd go to the back door and call, "We're looking for David!" We'd call "Dave!" until he'd come out. We were close. We played together. We went to school together. We even did some studying together . . . although I didn't do a lot of that. But I did some. That's all gone today.

Movies were a relatively big thing. You could go to a movie for ten cents in those days. Generally, we'd go to the Fort Theatre. I thought *Wuthering Heights*, in 1939, was a great movie.

The radio was also a big thing. We had a radio and listened to it regularly. We'd listen to the news. I don't recall who the newscaster was. And *Fibber McGee and Mollie* was a favorite. Humor, you know.

Through the Depression, jobs for women were extremely hard to get. So, my mother, during the Depression, was strictly a mother. She did everything around the house. Well, almost everything. There were eleven years between me and my oldest brother, and Mom used us kids, to the greatest extent she could, to help her with the cleaning. She also did the washing, dusting, and a lot of the cleaning and gardening.

Dad was busy with the real estate business, but he did help with laundry. Laundry was a big thing. When Mom did laundry, she used an old wooden tub with a gravity drain. There was an agitator that looked like a milk stool—a three-legged agitator, which oscillated, down in the water. There were wringers that you ran the clothes through. They sat atop the tubs. You would run clothes from one tub through the wringers and into a second tub for rinsing. All the laundry got hung out in the yard to dry. There were no dryers.

All through my life, our house was heated with coal. We shoveled coal. We'd stoke it up at night and put the "check" on. The check minimized the draft, and would keep the fire burning all night. You'd go down two or three times during the day to fill it up and keep it burning. Unless you put the check on, in an eight-hour night you'd have to go down a time or two. The check would keep the draft down. It kept a minimal fire burning.

To fill our coal bin, a truck would come in and dump the coal into a type of chute, which went into an open basement window. That's how they filled up the coal bin. When the coal truck was almost empty, the coal didn't get a good gravity flow out of a dump truck, so they had to shovel out whatever coal was left in the truck to get it into the chute.

We had an icebox. Later we had a refrigerator, probably just before the war years. Before that, during most of my young life, we had an icebox. It had a grade door, level with the ground coming in, and there was a gravity drain in the bottom of the box which drained into a basement sink. As the ice melted, the water would drain out.

As I recall, the ice wagon was pulled by horses. To save on gasoline, they even used horses into the war years. It was not uncommon to have horse-drawn wagons in those days. Even after the war, when a new house was built in the neighborhood, the basement was often dug out with horse-drawn scrapers.

I started school at Lincoln School. My days at the old Lincoln School were rather routine. School every day. You paid attention to the teacher. I think they did a pretty good job. I went to the old high school after junior high.

When I was a kid, I had a terrible allergy. It would come on in the fall of the year, as the ragweed pollinated. During the Depression, there were many undeveloped lots, so pollen was really a problem. The theaters by then were air-conditioned, and that was another reason we went to them. You'd get into that air-conditioning, and your nose would be cured of its ragweed problem. You could also get relief on the old Kauke ferry on the river. For a nickel, you could stay on it all day and ride it back and forth across the river. Fred Kauke, who had the boat-yard, moved into the house to the south of us.

CHAPTER 12

I CAN RECALL THAT DURING THE STRIKE THERE WAS A HOUSE, JUST DOWN THE STREET FROM US, THAT WAS BOMBED. WE WERE AWAKENED IN THE MIDDLE OF THE NIGHT WITH THIS BIG EXPLOSION AND WITH OUR HOUSE SHAKING.

- JEANETTE ROSS -
(Born September 1, 1926)

My name is Jeanette Ross. I was born on September 1, 1926. I just had my ninety-fourth birthday.

My mother came from Scotland with her family when she was about eight years old. Her maiden name was Jones.

My dad was born in England. He had come to the United States as a teenager, alone, after he finished school. He had two older brothers who were already here. Later, he went back to England, but then there were unsettling rumors of a coming war involving England, so he returned to the United States, and he enlisted in the United States Army. He was in his early twenties. Then, as a result of his enlistment, he got his United States citizenship. That was a perk of joining the army. I learned that a lot later. He didn't end up going overseas in World War I. He spent the first part of his enlistment as an instructor at Camp Taylor, in Kentucky. My mother and dad were married in 1918, while he was still in the military.

In my early years, I lived in Taylorville, Illinois. My dad was a coal miner. So were my mother's dad, and my mother's brothers. They had earlier lived in the little town of Witt, which was southeast of Springfield. They had moved to Taylorville because of employment opportunities in the coal mines. There had been a mine in Witt that closed, and that is why they all moved to Taylorville.

While we lived in Taylorville, I can remember that there was a coal miners' strike. The union called itself the Progressive Miners of America.*

If I recall, the miners' union was new at the time. I don't know whether the union was just trying to form itself, or whether it was striking to get better working conditions. I have no memory of what had gone on before that. But anyway, there was a big strike. It got very nasty and rather dangerous. My recollection is that they called in the National Guard to keep the peace between the strikers and the non-strikers, and whomever else was involved. That meant my father was unemployed because he was a strong union person and was involved with this strike.

I recall that during the strike there was a house, just down the street from us, that was bombed. We were awakened in the middle of the night by this big explosion. Our house was shaking. I don't know who did the bombing or whose house got bombed. I just knew that it happened as the result of the strike and the hostility that had taken over the town at the time. I don't recall going to look at what had happened to the house that had been bombed. I just know that it made a big noise and woke us up in the middle of the night.

And I can remember that during this time, people carried guns. I can recall going to somebody's house at night and knocking at the front door for some reason, and seeing this man come down the stairs with a gun in his hand. He was not going to answer the door without a gun. It

---

* The Progressive Miners of America was a coal miners' union organized in 1932 in downstate Illinois. It was formed in response to a 1932 contract proposal negotiated by United Mine Workers' President John L. Lewis, which reduced wages from a previous rate of $6.10 per day to $5.00 per day.

was scary for a kid. It scared the bejeebers out of me. And even though I generally knew what was going on, I never actually saw a coal mine.

I can also remember—and I don't know what precipitated it—that one of my uncles ended up in jail during the strike for picketing or something. And although he spent only that night in jail, it was a shocker. Looking back, I can see that a lot of good came out of that union activity: the forty-hour work week, overtime pay, paid vacations, and everything that we take for granted in today's world. It wouldn't have happened if those people back then hadn't put their lives on the line to make unions strong. All of those things that later became law, did so because of those miners and the whole labor movement. It made an impression that has lasted.

I can also recall that Dad and his friends used to go out to cut timber to get wood to burn in their furnaces for heat. Apparently, they could not afford to buy coal at that time. One day, he came home very upset. One of his friends had been killed by a falling tree. It stuck in my mind that it was really dangerous to cut trees down if you weren't a skilled lumberman.

My three uncles, my mother's brothers, were all miners. They all quit the mines at this time and moved to Michigan to seek work in the auto industry. They left Illinois forever. In those days, there were many coal mines throughout southern Illinois.

And I can recall that it was not unusual for men who were looking for food to knock on the door. My mom would always fix a plate of food, whether it was mealtime or not, and give it to the hungry men. They weren't invited in because my mother did not know who they were, but they would sit on the back steps and eat their meal. They were always gracious. They would say, "Thank you," and then they would go on their ways. I can remember my parents saying that "our house must have some kind of welcoming sign on it." It seemed like it was visited frequently. Perhaps our house was marked as someplace to come. Mom would always fix food for whomever knocked on the door. I don't think that it was an unusual thing for people to just hit the road, hop a train, and do whatever they did.

I don't know whether my parents were buying our home at the time or not. But I do know my grandparents left Taylorville and went back to this little town of Witt, where they had lived previously. At that time, we moved from the house in which we had been living into the house in which my grandparents had been living. Long after, I finally figured out that if they were buying these houses during the Depression, and if they were without money, they probably just left it and lost whatever little investment they had in their homes.

While we were living there, we got our first telephone. I don't know how long before we got our phone, that people began getting telephones. I must have been about six-years-old or in first grade at the time. Getting the phone was really exciting. I don't recall using it, but I know it was there. I went to first grade in Taylorville.

I can't remember the first house that we lived in in Taylorville, but I can remember the house that my grandparents had that we moved into. As I said, when they went back to Witt, we moved into their house in Taylorville. The big thing that I remember best about that house was that when you came out the front door there were two steps going down to the sidewalk. One day when I came out, I fell down the stairs and hit my head on a little rock on the sidewalk. My head began to bleed, and it bled and bled. I can recall being put into the car with a towel around my head to go to the doctor. But my head stopped bleeding on the way to the doctor, so we went back home.

The house was like a two-story bungalow. I remember the hallway. There was a living room, a dining room, and a kitchen all on one side of the hallway. And there was a bathroom and there were bedrooms on the other side of the hallway. In the back, there were stairs going up to the second floor. I didn't spend much time upstairs; I must have had a bedroom downstairs.

At the time, a cousin, who was still in high school, was living with us. He had lived with my grandparents in that house before they moved back to Witt. He was going to Taylorville High School. He stayed with us after we moved in.

That house in Taylorville had indoor plumbing. It also had electricity and central heating. I can remember that because Dad had to cut wood for the furnace.

We lived in that Taylorville house, but only for a short time. Then we also moved back to Witt, where my grandparents had gone earlier. I went to second grade through junior high school there in Witt. I was seven at the time we moved back.

At first, we lived in a rented house. And there was a bit of a shock when we moved in. There was no indoor plumbing! The house in Witt didn't have indoor plumbing at that time! I am guessing that there wasn't even a sewer system in that town. That came a bit later. Nor did the house in Witt have central heat. It had a heating stove in the living room. We would awaken in the morning to the sound of my dad shaking the grate to get the ashes to fall down so he could add wood or coal to build a new fire. In the kitchen, we had—as did all the houses in Witt that I can remember—an old-fashioned cast-iron cook stove that both cooked and provided heat.

To take a bath, we had a tub, but you had to pour water into it. It wasn't connected to a water source. You had to carry water to fill it, which you had heated on the cook stove, which was always burning, winter, summer, spring, or fall. You'd do the same to do the laundry. We did, however, have electricity at Witt. For bathroom facilities, we had an outhouse, with two holes, if I remember correctly. Everybody had outhouses. They were horrible!

Then a little later, when I was in elementary school, we bought a house that we lived in for the rest of the time that I was in school there.

I always felt my dad was ahead of his time. I felt he was really smart. He read all of the time. He was very good with figures, and because he was so active with the union movement, he got a job with the union and traveled to communities all over the southern half of Illinois. When I was little, I didn't know where all the towns were that Dad would mention. But later, as I got older, when I'd travel around southern Illinois and when we went to the little towns, I got to know where they were, all the way down to Carbondale, Illinois. And I could recall my dad mentioning them.

Traveling wasn't easy in those days. Cars weren't air conditioned and had no radios. Because Dad traveled so much, he needed a decent car. In those days, the "going color" of cars was black. And I think he bought a new black Chevy sedan for $650. I can remember when he bought It. I was ten at the time. So, it would've been in 1936. Most cars in those days were sedans; you didn't have many choices. I remember my parents having a conversation about buying a car. I can remember them discussing that they would have a new car, and not many of the people around us would have a car. "What would the neighbors think? Would they think we were rich because we had a new car?"

My mother was a stay-at-home mother. All mothers were in those days. She stayed home and took care of the house and us kids, and fed us.

We always had a garden. I think Dad liked to garden. We raised sweet corn, cabbage, cauliflower, green beans, carrots, radishes, and onions. And my dad liked peas, so we always had peas. I didn't especially care about peas, but we always had peas. Maybe that was because I had to shell them. My mother canned, and made jams and jellies for us.

I was young enough during the Depression that it didn't affect me very much. I always had a family. I always had a home. And we always had food. I had both a sister, Laura Ann, and a brother, Warren, who were both older than I was. They might have been a bit more affected than I. I think people who were a little older were affected more by the Depression. I had older cousins and friends that I remained in contact with throughout my life. They never got over the need to have things— to have possessions. I've always felt I had enough. I've always felt very fortunate to have had "enough." I never felt "deprived."

My mom sewed for my sister and me. Mom liked to sew. I always had clothes. She was pretty good. I learned to sew on her old treadle sewing machine. I still have it, and I still have my father's old desk, in my home today. They were the only things that I wanted out of my parents' house. Dad's desk was "Dad's territory," and it was off limits for us kids. I think he paid the bills and kept receipts there. It was always off limits. Even after my parents were gone, my brother and I agreed that we felt funny opening it. It was Dad's! Even then, it seemed to be off limits. I have kept it all these years. It's not a valuable thing. It's just something I like.

When I got a little older—and my kids cannot believe this – I used to babysit for twenty-five cents a night. Later in the forties, when I was in college, I worked for fifty cents an hour.

When my brother Warren graduated from high school, my parents couldn't afford to send him to college. So, in 1937, he got a job in a little store, and he worked for a dollar a day. It was a little local dry goods store that sold things like shoes and clothes. I'm sure it was not very exciting for a young guy.

I think my sister was always a wannabe hair dresser. She loved to mess with people's hair. I used to babysit when I got old enough. When she got old enough, she used to go and set people's hair in the neighborhood. She probably got a quarter or a dime for that. I think she did it because she didn't like helping to dust and clean house.

We had a tabletop radio with a rounded top. When the news came on, all other operations stopped and everybody listened to the news. The radio was at Grandma's house in Witt. I can't remember a radio in Taylorville. When I was a kid, I listened to all the after-school serials, like *Jack Armstrong*. And you could send away for things, but you had to send cereal box tops. And you'd get this, or that. All the kids listened to them, and we'd talk about them at school. I listened to whatever came on after school. I think there was one called *Captain Midnight*. That's what I remember.

And there was a phonograph. I think they called it a gramophone. We were just little kids, and it seemed like it was big and tall. You wound it up with a handle. The record went around and around. I don't know where the sound came out. There was a lid that covered the mechanism. To play it, you lifted the lid and put the records on.

We went to the movies. We had no movie theater in town, but we went to a neighboring little town called Nokomis. We saw *Snow White* there. That was a big deal. I was probably eight or ten at the time.

Today people go to shop in and visit Chicago. When I was a kid, going to Springfield was a big thing. The shopping district there was the downtown district. I remember being intrigued with a store that had a mezzanine balcony. They would put the money in a container, and it would shoot up to the mezzanine. They'd make the change on the mezzanine, and then they shot the container back down. Pneumatic—like they have at banks now. They had that in the store then. You'd give the money to the clerk, and she would shoot the money and the ticket up to the mezzanine, and they shot the change back down. I thought that was really fun. The store might have been Penney's.

And of course, they had Woolworth stores. We used to call them the "five and dimes." They always had a lady playing the piano! Her mission at Woolworths was to sell sheet music. I remember that when I was a little kid. I thought that was fascinating.

My dad died when he was fifty-three, in 1946. And they brought his body, and we had the wake in our living room.

CHAPTER 13

NOT EVERYBODY WAS POOR DURING THE DEPRESSION. . . . JOHN AND SUSANNE (DENKMANN) HAUBERG WERE VERY WEALTHY, BUT VERY GENEROUS. MRS. HAUBERG WAS ONE OF THE KINDEST PERSONS AROUND.

- KATHRYN "KATIE" FOULKES -
(Born July 28, 1921. Died February 1, 2021.)

I was born on July 28, 1921. I'm ninety-seven. I'll be ninety-eight in a couple months. I was an only child.

My great-grandparents had come down the Ohio River and up the Mississippi River on a flatboat from Pennsylvania in 1825. They arrived in Davenport in 1826. We lived in the house that my great-grandmother had built after they had arrived in Davenport, on what is now the corner of 13th and Grand: 702 E. 13th. I think it is now painted gray or white.

By the time we lived there, the house had electricity. We had everything, although we had to put in a hot water heater. There were double parlors, with beautiful woodwork.

My granddad was a great Masonic member, and he and some others played cards at the Masonic Temple. We really weren't deprived.

My father's business was Fleu's Battery Service. It was located at 5th Avenue and 20th Street in Rock Island, Illinois. Dad was in the business of recharging auto batteries and selling new batteries to people whose batteries could no longer be recharged. In those days, if you had a car, when the weather got very cold, you had to have your battery recharged to get the car started. He serviced a lot of the businesses around Rock Island that used trucks and autos. Besides servicing the batteries, Dad did some mechanical work. He also sold tires. Prior to the Depression, Dad's business had been quite good, but during the Depression, his business went way down.

If the Depression wasn't bad enough, to make things worse, the city of Rock Island closed 20th Street for a whole year. That was the main access to my father's business. People had to drive around to 6th Avenue or 4th Avenue to 21st Street, and come across 5th Avenue. It ruined Dad's business. He finally just closed the doors. His equipment went to the Rock Island Transfer Company. Its owners were very close friends of ours. When Dad's business closed, many people lost their jobs.

After his business closed, he just did all sorts of things. He did some sales, but he finally went to work for Sieg in Davenport, and worked there until he died. He was head of the price department there. Sieg sold auto parts.

When the war came, dad went to the Arsenal. When he interviewed, one of the women there said he wasn't qualified to work there. The next day, he met the man whom he knew was in charge of W-1 over there. They met on the street. Dad said, "I guess I'm not going to work for you." The man asked, "Why not?" Dad said, "Well, the girl said I wasn't capable." The man responded, "Report to work in the morning." Dad worked there all through the war.

During the Depression, my mother was a homemaker. She had previously worked for old Dr. Arp—Dr. A. Henry Arp. She had earlier run his medical office, for perhaps five or six years. I remember her saying he was a very good doctor, but "if you could get around his temper, you were lucky." She told the story of how he got mad, pulled the phone out of the office wall, and threw it out the window! But she somehow survived. She managed his office. She was his right hand. He just had a horrible temper. His son, Louis, who was also an MD, used to say, "I've got a temper, but it doesn't match my dad's at all." They did surgery. They did everything in that office. They did early X-rays, and they were all a bit exposed in those days. Dr. Arp's second son was also an MD.

During the Depression, my dad owned a little farm out on 30th Street, near 25th Avenue, Rock Island. Today, 25th Avenue almost runs into what was our farm's driveway. There is still a house there. It's now painted dark red.

Our farm was only a couple of acres. We were very lucky we had it. The food we raised on that little farm kept three families going during the Depression—my dad's family, my mother's family, and our family. The men farmed it on Sundays, and we all ate from it. On our farm, we had eleven apple trees, cherry trees, grapes, plums, and everything you can think of that you could grow. We had a family garden there with potatoes, corn, green beans, and everything. We owned the front half of the land; another family had the back half. They raised and sold vegetables off it.

Other people were not so lucky. My closest girlfriend's father had a drug store at 4th and Scott Street in Davenport. He had to close it. After that, they really had a hard time. Those were hard days. My friend told me that her dad went to the Davenport city dump to find what he could for food—something that they could cook and eat. During the Depression, many people opened their homes and rented rooms to people who needed a place to stay.

In those days, the street cars were very popular. People simply couldn't afford cars.

And then there was Quinlan's Ferry. Bill Quinlan ran his ferry boat between Davenport and Rock Island. In the 1930s, the Centennial Bridge between Rock Island and Davenport didn't exist (construction on it only began in 1938, and it wasn't completed until July of 1940). Of course, you could get between Rock Island and Davenport by using the Government Bridge, but you could run into a pretty big delay if its swing span was open so a boat could get through the lock.

If the Government Bridge was open and my father needed tires or parts, he'd take the ferry to Davenport where his supplier, the John P. Hand Company, had its warehouse.

Bill Quinlan would just put Dad's truck on the ferry and take him over and back. The boat was big enough that others on the boat would not even know that my dad's truck was on the boat with them. It was kind of hidden at the end of the boat. Dad and Bill Quinlan were good friends. It was a big boat; they could get a lot of people on that boat.

I can remember taking the ferry. It was fun. It cost a nickel. My mother would park the car in Rock Island, and we'd take the ferry. Then you could shop in Davenport, as well as in Rock Island. You could ride back and forth all day for a nickel. The ferry's second floor featured a dance floor and bar. You could go up there and dance. I seem to recall that they sold near-beer at the bar.

For a while we lived on 8th Avenue and 34th Street, near Augustana College.

After that, we lived at 1020 20th Street. Mrs. Rink's father had built two duplicate houses on 20th Street with high attics. The high tower on our house was my playhouse. Well, it was my playhouse when I was seven.

The people in our neighborhood, 20th Street up to 30th Street, were good about sending their kids to school. The area from 25th Street to 30th Street was largely an Irish and German neighborhood. I went first to Eugene Field School, and then to Lincoln School for third grade. It was on 7th Avenue at 22nd Street. It has since been torn down.

Later, we moved to Davenport, because my father's family came from there.

Not everybody was poor during the Depression. My parents came to know the Hauberg family through our church, the Broadway Church. My dad was treasurer of the church until 1936 or 1937. John and Susanne (Denkmann) Hauberg were very wealthy, but very generous. Mrs. Susanne Hauberg was one of the kindest persons around. She did everything that was necessary to help the church.

She also saw to it that there was money in the Rock Island Bank to keep it afloat. She sent to Chicago for the money so that the bank had funds, so that our people could make withdrawals if they wanted some of their own money from the bank.

She also kept the Rock Island Plow Company going. She kept a stove company running, too. She did what she did so that the men had a place to work and sources of income. She also put up a building and hired a woman to manage it to assist the Belgian immigrants. Few people realized all that she did.

My folks belonged to the Blackhawk Hiking Club, which her husband, John Hauberg, started in 1921. I went on hikes for five years in striped overalls, and Mr. Hauberg pulled me and another young girl along beside him when we had a leader with long legs that covered a lot of territory. Mr. Hauberg also somehow arranged a tour for us of the locks and dams as they were being constructed in the Mississippi River. We were down at the bottom of the river. It was kind of spooky, and I couldn't wait to get out of there. But there I was!

When Mrs. Hauberg would invite us to the house after a hike, we always went. Mr. Hauberg would throw his overcoat, with all the burrs and everything, across her gilded chairs with the needlepoint, and Mrs. Hauberg and my mother would look at each other and laugh.

CHAPTER 14

YOU SHOULD ALSO MENTION IN YOUR BOOK HOW IMPORTANT SOME OF THE ROCK ISLAND WEALTHY FAMILIES WERE TO THE COMMUNITY.

- CAROLYN HOLMGRAIN -

I was born in 1934, so I don't have a great many personal memories of the Great Depression. I was born in Missouri. We moved up here in 1938. We lived on the second floor of an apartment building on Spring Street in Davenport, Iowa.

Ardo* did not talk to you about the hot summers in 1934 and 1936. They were miserably hot. The neighborhood people would get together in the backyards under sprinklers.

Our house was an old, Victorian-style house. At night, we'd go up to the third-floor attic of our home and open the windows on each end to let the breeze go through. The kids would then go up in the attic. But many people in apartment buildings had nowhere to go to cool off. So, they would go out and camp in Blackhawk State Park. There was a valley out there, where the Rock Island Family Athletic Center is now located. It would be cooler there, and people camped there in the valley.

---

* Carolyn Holmgrain refers to her husband, Ardo Homlgrain, whose memories appear above in Chapter 12.

They took their old Indian blankets. The valley would be just full of people out there, just trying to survive the heat. It was so miserably hot.

The Horst family had a tract of land south of 31st Avenue between 12th and 14th Streets which they used as a camping area called Seven Acres. People would also camp there to escape the heat.

Before my sister's birth—I believe it was in the spring of 1938—there was a serious outbreak of the measles.

The children downstairs were already in grade school, and they brought the measles home—the "hard measles," as they were called. There was the three-day kind, and there was the bad kind. Mother and I were terribly, terribly sick. At the time, my mother was pregnant.

The measles affected my mother's eyes, and she could not stand the light. For that reason, quilts were hung over our windows so that no light could come in—because the light hurt my mother's eyes so badly. She couldn't stand for any light to come in. It hurt her eyes so badly.

Mother and I eventually recovered. But my mother, who as I said was pregnant with my sister, gave birth to my sister later that September. Sadly, my sister was born deaf in one ear. She was deaf in that ear all her life. The doctors attributed her deafness to the measles.

You should also mention in your book how important some of the Rock Island wealthy families were to the community. I'm speaking mainly of John Hauberg and his wife Susanne Denkman Hauberg.

John Hauberg was an attorney. The couple built both the YMCA and YWCA for the children of the community. John Hauberg was devoted to helping young boys make good. For that purpose, he started a Boys' Club. John Hauberg was also a historian. He became especially interested in preserving Quad Cities' history. In his old age, he came to realize that if it was going to get done, he would have to do it himself. So, the basement of his mansion became the first Rock Island County Historical Museum. To preserve the history of Rock Island County, he took and collected pictures and accounts of the "old settlers" and their children who were still alive.

During the Depression, young women were coming into the cities from the countryside to become secretaries and to get jobs, so they needed a place to live that was respectable. Their families all wanted a nice place where their girls could stay as single women. So, the Lend-a-Hand Club was built by the King's Daughters. It was on Main Street in Davenport. It was lovely. It was a dormitory. Downstairs on the main floor were the clubrooms. And there was a swimming pool in the basement. It was a handsome brick building, which has since been torn down.

CHAPTER 15

MY FATHER DIDN'T GO TO ANY CHURCH, BUT HE WOULD STAND OUT IN THE YARD AND TELL YOU THERE WAS ONLY ONE GOD, AND HE WOULD SHOW ME WHERE HE WAS.

- JOYCE MEYER JACQUIN -
(Born April 26, 1926. Died January 5, 2022.)

My name is Joyce Meyer Jacquin. I am ninety-four years old. I was born on April 26, 1926.

I have only moved once in my life. I moved from my family home to where I live now. I was born in the Fruitland Addition of Moline, Illinois. The Fruitland Addition lies south of Moline and south of Blackhawk Road, which in those days was at the southern end of Moline. Our house is still there. The area wasn't built up then; it was all country.

At first, our house in Fruitland was just four little rooms and a front porch. I don't recall exactly when my dad had it remodeled, but I was in grade school at the time. That was when we got electricity, bathrooms, and running water.

Before that we had to take our baths in a washtub. We'd bathe once a week in the kitchen in the old scrub tub in which mom did the washing. The water was heated on the old cook stove, and our house was heated by the cook stove and a coal stove that sat in the living room. You could see the fire in it. That's the way the house was heated until we remodeled.

Then we added two bedrooms downstairs, and a bedroom for my brother, Edward, upstairs. He was an electric train nut, and half of the upstairs was turned into his train room. He had all the latest models of Lionel electric trains. He had beautiful trains and kept them into later life. He had a train layout even after he married.

My brother was two years older than I. He was born on August 24, 1924 and he later became "Meyer's Tree Farm." He took over the nursery from a man named Frank, who was my dad's friend. Mr. Frank had no family. When he got old, he wanted to sell the business, and by then, my brother was old enough to buy it.

I went to Maple Grove Grade School, which sat along the north side of Blackhawk Road, just below Prospect Park. Maple Grove was an old, two-story school. My father was president of the school board, and they built the new Maple Grove School to replace the old one. I was in eighth grade when the new school was finished, and I was therefore in the first class that graduated from the new school. The old school bell is still there. It was given to my dad when they tore down the old two-story school. The new Maple Grove School building is still there, but it is now used by a church. The old bell is still there, sitting there on a post.

During the years when I was in grade school, I had only two teachers. One teacher taught four grades, and the other teacher taught the other four grades. Mrs. Greenwood taught first grade through fourth grade, and Mrs. Persinger, who was originally from England, taught the other four grades. Both were very nice. My dad was friends with them. They were both married.

My father worked for John Deere. He was a blacksmith. His father had come over from Germany, and had worked at Deere. My brother also worked for Deere. And I worked for ten years at Deere. I started there in November of 1943 after graduating from high school.

My dad also worked at the Butterworth Farm, which was owned by the Wymans and the Butterworths. They owned the John Deere Company. Their farm was situated on the hill, up above and north of Blackhawk Road. It ran east for a couple blocks from what would be 8th Street. Dad helped them grow all the vegetables that they used during the Depression. That farm is really what kept us alive. They were very kind, and allowed my dad to take some of the vegetables and fruits. When he wasn't working at Deere, Dad would go up to the farm and work in the gardens there. That's where they grew all the vegetables and fruits used by the Wymans and the Butterworths. In those days, the farm was known as Orchard Hill Farm, because in those days there were many apple trees on that farm. And they also raised chickens and pigs. I don't think they had cows. There was a farmer down below Blackhawk Road who had all the cows.

My dad also had a little flower business. That's my favorite story. He started growing irises, and then he added dahlias. He had mostly perennials, but some annuals. Very few annuals.

He sold them to people on the side. It was another business that he had. He raised them by our home. We had three lots at the time, and he raised them there. That was a lot of land at the time. When I was a child, I thought it was a lot of ground; now, when I look at it, it appears so tiny.

I remember, when I was small, how Mrs. Wyman and Mrs. Butterworth would come out to see Dad's flowers. They lived in the great mansions off 7th Street. Their chauffeurs would bring them out, and I would look at them out the window. I was never allowed to go out while they were there. But I can remember the chauffeurs opening the car doors. They would then take their hats off and get out. They were always very well-dressed. My dad would go out to greet them. He would be in his old work clothes. They would take off their gloves and shake hands with him, and then go out in the garden with him. He would explain all the flowers to them. Dad furnished a lot of the perennials that they planted around their homes. They, of course, had their own gardeners, but my dad would work with them.

Mrs. Wyman lived in what is now known as the Deere-Wyman House. The Butterworth Home is now called Butterworth Center. They are no longer private homes, but are rather like civic centers, devoted to meetings of not-for-profit groups and educational and cultural events. Of course, I didn't spend any time there. Later in life, Dad would drive by and show me the mansions. But that was it. His relationship was strictly business.

Up the high hill and to the north of Maple Grove school is what is now the Quad City Music Guild Building. It was originally built in the early 1900s by the Tri-City Railway Company. When I was little, it was known as the Prospect Park Pavilion. I believe it was originally built as an old Chautauqua house. It sits at the south end of Prospect Park. When I was a child, it was just a big empty building. There were doors on three sides, rather like garage doors, that they would raise up in the summer. We could play in there. In those days the building was all open inside. I think they used to have a lot of picnics in there. And there were swings up there on that hill. We played there during the summer, but when we were in school, the Maple Grove kids were not allowed to go inside the building and play there, or use the swings. We had to use what the school provided us below the hill.

To the northwest of that Pavilion, the land fell off steeply, down to a lagoon. We used to ice skate on the lagoon at Prospect Park in the winter. At that time, there was a bridge across the lagoon, and they had a building in the middle on the bridge. In the summer we used to swim in the lagoon—in the shallow end. I can't remember if the building on the bridge was a bath house where you could change. When we went, we always had our suits on already. During school hours, we could not go to the lagoon; we couldn't leave the school property. They were quite strict.

Northeast of the lagoon, but still in the park, the land rose a bit and on the hill there was another building. It was an open, two-story pavilion. We never used it much, but there were a lot of picnics there. That pavilion is a very old building. Today, it's a favorite place for weddings. It had a roof, so you were protected from the sun while you were there. And it was the one place where you could get a drink of water. They had a water fountain there.

Because we lived in Fruitland, we had to walk north across Blackhawk Road to swim or skate in Prospect Park.

When we wanted to take the street car, we had to walk north from Fruitland, past the lagoon, and up a lane to 16th Street. We could catch the trolley there to go downtown or to the high school. We'd catch the trolley where the WQAD-TV building presently sits. At first, there was a trolley line, and later a bus. The trolley was still there when I was going to Moline High School. I graduated from there in 1943. It cost a nickel to take the street car from Prospect Park to the High School.

The trolley ran north from where WQAD-TV now sits on 16th Street. It then ran north on 16th Street to where 15th Street and 16th Street came together. It then continued north on 15th Street. The old high school faced east onto 16th Street. We'd get off on 15th Street, behind the high school, and then we had to walk east up the hill along a pathway that led to the back steps of the high school.

As a child, my early life was very simple. We had our dolls and our bikes. Our bikes were our lifesavers. We rode all over. Later, as we got older, we even rode to Blackhawk State Park which was along Blackhawk Road in Rock Island. We never thought anything of riding all that way. But there weren't as many cars in those days on the road for us to worry about. During the summer, as we got older, we did a lot of biking. We thought we were lucky to have two-wheel bikes.

And we'd also walk down to the Rock River. We walked because there were no roads going down to it. But really, the creek was our main playground. When the water was good, we'd block up the creek and have a place to swim. We played at that creek a lot. It was a main source of our entertainment. There weren't many girls where we lived in those days, so I mainly played with the boys. The neighbors, up the street a couple of houses, had two sons, Glen and Ken. The four of us would play together.

The only girls at all nearby were up at the top of the hill. The Tunnicliffs had a daughter, Joanne, whom they called Joan. They lived in the first house at the top of the hill on the left side of 14th Street. It was the first nearby house to have a telephone. They actually had a phone booth in their home. You'd hold the phone up to your ear, and when you were done, you had to make sure it clamped down. I can remember going up there to see the phone. And I'd go up to see Joan, but that was a long walk when we were little.

There was a stone wall that had been built north of Blackhawk Road, opposite from where you would go south to enter Fruitland. We used to climb that wall all the time to walk north up 14th Street to get to Prospect Park. It was a shortcut.

There was a farm near us. The farmhouse, which is still there, was on the south side of Blackhawk Road, and the farm was on the north side, up the hill. Today it is hard to imagine how the area looked when I was young. Then, it was all hills. When I ride there today, it's hard to imagine the hillside that was there when I was a child. How different it is now!

When I was young, there was a cattle barn to the west of our house near the creek, which is now along 10th Street. Now there's a bridge that goes over it. From our house, as you faced north, there was the horse barn. Then, if you walked a little further north, there was the milk shed. Then, west of the creek was the big barn where the cattle were kept and milked. When I was a child, it all seemed so big to me; now the area all seems so small. It doesn't seem possible! The farm belonged to Bud Prosser. He lived with his mother. His sister was a teacher.

When I was young, I used to sit on top of one of our sheds and watch Mr. Prosser plow his back cornfields. At first, he plowed with his horses. One day, as I was sitting on our shed watching him plow with two horses, one of the horses dropped over dead. I can still remember that. I could point out to you where it happened, but there are houses there now. But I can still remember the horse dying. Mr. Prosser just unhooked it and waited for my dad to come home that night. My dad took care of the horse. They probably just dug a hole and put the horse in it.

Then, as I got a little older, I used to go up and help Mr. Prosser, because I loved being around the farm. Then, by the time I was twelve or thirteen, he'd let me drive the tractor. I did almost all the plowing of his ground for him. Being around farming was my childhood life. But he wouldn't let me drive the horses. When he plowed with the horses, he'd let me ride with him, but he wouldn't let me do anything with the horses.

To the east of us was the Midvale Farm. It was a dairy farm at the intersection of 16th Street and Blackhawk Road. It was at the bottom of the 16th Street hill. Half of Midvale Farm was north of Blackhawk Road and the other half was south of it. The south end of 16th Street would've run into Midvale Farm. In those days 16th Street stopped at the bottom of the hill. It was a dairy farm that delivered milk to the Quad Cities. The big old white barn that used to sit at the southeast corner of the intersection was the Midvale Farm dairy barn.

The first car that I can remember us having was a 1936 Plymouth. It was gray. My brother was more interested in the car than I was.

In those days, we had the Roxy Theater in Moline. It was at the corner of 15th Street and 15th Avenue. It cost a nickel to get in. On Saturday afternoons, somebody would take us to the theater. My brother, Edward, was a *Tarzan* fan, and I loved Shirley Temple. In fact, I was a Shirley Temple nut. I had a lot of her books with the paper dolls. For very little money, you could get a scrap book, with a stiff, paper Shirley Temple doll on the front cover. Her clothes would be inside. You could spend hours playing with paper dolls. I did that a lot.

We had a radio, but I can't remember when we first got it.

And my mother taught me to crochet and to embroider at a very young age. I loved crocheting. And as I am sitting here, I am putting a granny Afghan together. I just finished creating all the squares, and now I have to put them together. It's been my lifesaver, later in life.

My mother was Catholic. My father didn't go to any church, but he would stand out in the yard and tell you there was only one God, and he would show me where he was. It was his belief that everything else became possible through God. He loved his flowers; he loved his vegetable gardens. He would give something to every customer who would come out. He had a lot of good customers who'd come out to buy his flowers. He'd always had rhubarb, or something in the garden that he would give them to take home. He was a "yard guy;" he loved being outside. Now,

I look at the ground and wonder, "How did he raise everything that he gave away?" But he had a way.

And I can also remember how my mother made strawberry jam. We'd pick the strawberries, and my mother would put them in big flat bowls and cover them with sugar. Then she would set the bowls in the sun out on the wash bench. She'd cover the bowls with a big piece of glass, and the sun would cook those strawberries and make jam. I can't recall any more details, but that's how she made her strawberry jam. It was wonderful! She'd put her jam in Mason jars, seal them with hot wax, and screw on the tops. Then she would put the jars down in the cellar. The cellar had a dirt floor and there were shelves. She'd put the jars on shelves. It was cool in the cellar all the time. The jam would keep all winter.

Mom's washing machine—the one that I can remember—was a Maytag. It had a metal basin that had the wringers on it. She got that washing machine only after our house had been remodeled and electrified. Once we got electricity, she could plug it in. She kept the Maytag washer on our back porch, which had been added on when we remodeled the house.

Before she got the Maytag, she had a washboard. I can remember watching her use it. I can remember the washboard, the bench, and the tubs. To be honest, before she got the Maytag, I don't know how she washed all the diapers that had to be washed!

I feel very fortunate. I had such a good life.

CHAPTER 16

ONCE MOM GOT THAT DRIVER'S LICENSE, HER WHOLE LIFE CHANGED. BEFORE THAT— LIKE MOST FARM WOMEN—SHE SPENT MOST OF HER LIFE AT HOME, OR AT THEIR CHURCH. THEY ALL DID.

- KAY CONWAY CORRIGAN -
(Born May 25, 1925)

My name is Kay Conway Corrigan. I was born on May 25, 1925, on a farm, south of Reynolds, Illinois. They always told me that that was the year the corn froze off.

After I was born, there were six of us in my family: Mom and Dad, Jim, Tom, Mary, and me. Then six years later, my brother Chuck came along. He was my little doll. He was the neatest little guy. I was always dressing him up. He had a beautiful soprano voice, and my mother would play the piano and he would sing. She had been a music teacher. Chuck was always asked to entertain at all sorts of events.

We had a nice big home. It is still standing. I believe that my grandfather had built it for my grandmother. It had four bedrooms upstairs. We also had a bathroom with running water upstairs. That was most unusual in those days. And we had electric lights—ceiling lights—which were powered by a system up in the attic. It was called a Delco[1] system; it ran off batteries in the attic. To turn the lights on, you pushed a button—not a switch like we have today. But then when electricity came into the country, my mother signed up immediately.

Besides having that bathroom upstairs, we had a half-bath downstairs. It had hot water. There was a hot water heater in the basement. We were more fortunate than a lot of people.

We also had a furnace in the basement—a coal furnace. They'd dump a whole bunch of coal into a room in the basement that was close to the furnace. We had to go down and shovel a couple of shovels of coal into the furnace every so often to keep the house warm.

I think when I was about eight, my mother got a freezer, so she didn't have to can. We had both a refrigerator and a freezer. But I can remember before we got the refrigerator, the iceman would come through the country, and we'd get a block of ice and put it in the icebox, which was out on the back porch.

As I remember, we always had a car. It was a Chrysler. My mother came from a little town in Iowa. We'd always drive out there at least once a year, and Dad would drive. We'd put the luggage on the running board, and I can remember that there was a little something that they strapped on the side of the car between the front door and the back door. That's where they put the luggage—on the running board. And then they hoped that it wouldn't rain. The town was Melrose, Iowa. The whole town was made up of Irish Catholics; there was only one non-Catholic family in the whole town. I don't know if it still exists. I haven't been out there for years. The biggest town nearby was Albia, Iowa.

I can remember when my mother learned to drive. I was probably about five at the time. They had to get a new car, but she wouldn't let my dad buy it until the fellow who was selling the car had taught her how to drive. I can remember sitting in the back seat of the car while she and the salesman drove around the countryside while she was getting her lessons. The new car was a Chrysler. And I even remember the name of the salesman: Cleve Minteer.

And that was the beginning of Mom becoming a "club lady." Once she got that driver's license, her whole life changed. Before that—like most farm women—she spent most of her life at home, or at church.

They all did. Once she could drive, she became a club lady in Aledo, Illinois. She was a woman who liked to get things done. She started Blue Cross Blue Shield there. That would have been around 1930.

Our little Catholic church was about a mile and a half from our house—St. Joseph's. I made my first Communion there. They had confessions before Mass, but I didn't really know how to make a confession. I took so long that Father would become anxious to get me out of the way so he could get on with the Mass. I think I thought that I was a bigger sinner than he did!

Everything in those days was in that little church. Sunday morning after Mass was really the social time for all the women. These farm ladies never saw anybody through the week. I can remember that in those days, you had to fast before you could go to Communion, and by the time Mass was over, we'd all be so hungry. But my mother would stand there chatting with everybody. That was her social time. Of course, they always had to pack a lunch for the priest, because he was fasting, too. Then, when we got home, we had the obligatory fried chicken dinner. It was a whole different type of life.

My parents or grandparents had donated the land for St. Joseph's Church and for the cemetery. It was a little country cemetery. I used to go out there on Memorial Day with twelve to fifteen bunches of flowers. So many friends we had known were buried out there! Our church was just a little country church sitting on the corner of the farm. That little old country church was torn down some years ago.

As I said above, we lived on a farm. I am not sure how big it was, but it was probably a couple hundred acres. They farmed it with a plow, hooked up to the horse. We didn't have a tractor then. Dad always had a hired man, who slept in one of the bedrooms upstairs. My nephew Jim, who is a judge, has the farm now.

My mother always had help. It was usually a hired girl, a teenaged girl, from the little town of Matherville. That girl, who was about fourteen, would stay at our home during the week and go home on the weekends. She helped mom with the laundry and helped to take care of us kids—so Mom didn't lose any of us! We had a dressmaker come to the house and make our clothes. I can remember standing on a chair while she hemmed my dress.

I can remember, before the Depression hit, we all got dressed and went to Carlson's studio in Aledo. We had our family picture taken there. I still have that picture.

Everything was just fine until the Depression hit in 1929. Then things changed. We didn't have the dressmaker come to the house any more. During the bad days of the Depression, we wore my brothers' castoff overalls with the knees worn out. But we wore them anyway. We had to wear shoes out of this old, blue denim "shoe bag." It contained shoes that the two children ahead of me had grown out of. When you outgrew your shoes, they went in that bag. Sometimes, I wore boy's shoes, and sometimes I wore my sister's shoes. But we saved the farm. That was the main object.

I went to a little grade school that was about three miles from our house. My sister and I rode a little pony, called Dolly, to school. My older brother, Jim, road a horse named Trixie. Jim was supposed to watch the two of us girls, but he'd leave us behind, crying because we barely knew where to go. The school closed when I graduated, because there were only perhaps five children still in the whole school.

I had an aunt who was a Dominican nun. My aunt was Sister Rose Marie Grady. She was my mother's sister. She ran what was a sort of boarding school in the little town of Philo, Illinois, some six miles southeast of Champaign. The school was called St. Joseph's Academy. It was both a grade school and a high school. It had opened in 1905 and closed during the Depression in 1938.

My brothers, Jim and Tom, went to boarding school down there. And my older sister, Mary, started there as a freshman, but she was a homebody and got very lonesome very quickly. She could hardly lift her head off her pillow. So, she got to come home and go to the local high school. St. Joseph's closed after there was a fire. Nobody knew how it started. So, my aunt had to close the school, and she sent my brothers and my sister back home. I can recall that my brother Jim, who was sixteen years-old, drove all the way back from Champaign to Reynolds. They then went to Reynolds High School in Reynolds, Illinois.

I was only at St. Joseph's once. The school was a brick building, which I remember as being two stories high. The girls slept in a dormitory, which was above the classrooms in the school; I vaguely recall that there were perhaps seven or eight classrooms. The boys slept over at the rectory with the priest. I am guessing that there weren't many boarders. But other kids also attended and went to classes. So, there must have been day students as well. And there were also kids there who didn't have parents. I never attended my aunt's boarding school.

After grade school, I went to Reynolds High School for a year. Then for my sophomore year, I went to another boarding school—the Villa de Chantal, in Rock Island. I wasn't surprised, because my older brothers had always gone to boarding school. I graduated from the Villa in 1943. Then I went on to college across the river, at Marycrest College in Davenport, Iowa, and graduated in 1946. Both of those schools are now closed.

The Villa de Chantal seemed like it was a school mostly for upper-class girls from the Quad Cities. The girls were all from rather affluent families. I was just a little farm girl. It was a big adjustment for me. But they were all so nice to me that I couldn't ask for a more welcoming group of girls.

When you came in on the first floor, there were offices. The kindergarten, the grade school rooms, and the dining room where we took our meals were also on the first floor. On the second floor there were the high school classrooms and the chapel. We boarders lived on the third floor. We had our own private rooms. Across the hall, there were double rooms with a bath in between them. And there was an infirmary at one end of the hall. You went there if you got sick. If you were running a fever, you got put there. We had what they called a "proctor," Mrs. McMann, who looked over us. She was an elocution teacher. She taught proper speech and manners. She lived on the third floor, too. She had a little apartment there.

There were probably twelve of us boarders. But the number would increase during the winter. Then, some of the day students would board, so they could stay in school while their parents wintered in Florida or some other warm place. They'd board them at the Villa.

I made two very good friends at the Villa. One was Pat Schierbrock. She later married Johnny Lujack, who played quarterback both for Notre Dame and the Chicago Bears. Pat was a year behind me. And then there was Jackie Tunnicliff who lived in Davenport. They were my very dear friends.

When it was time to eat, we came down to the dining room, on the first floor, and Mrs. McMann always sat at the head of the table. We put our napkins on our laps only after she had put her napkin in her lap. Then she would serve the soup out of a big soup tureen. Some of the boarder girls, who could not quite afford the tuition, served as waitresses. They waited the table, took away our soup dishes, and brought us our entrées. We couldn't leave until Mrs. McMann dismissed us. We were taught to follow directions.

We took the normal high school classes at the Villa. I took French as my foreign language. I couldn't speak it now if I had to. And, of course, there also was elocution.

One of the girls, who came from a very affluent family, had her own radio. I can remember that when the war broke out, we all gathered in her room and listened to how Pearl Harbor was attacked. We got to stay up past nine o'clock that night!

The grounds at the Villa were beautiful. You came in on 20th Street, and entered onto Rosary Drive, which was a little circular driveway, rather like a rosary. So, they always called it Rosary Drive. As you entered facing the building, we were on the right side, and the nuns had their quarters to the left side by the chapel. The principal had her office over there, too. And I can recall a tennis court.

Before the Depression, Christmas was a big deal. But when the Depression came, I didn't get very much at all in my stocking. I thought, *I must not have been a very good girl.* But all our family's money went toward saving the farm. We did save it, and as I said, it is still in the Conway family.

During the Depression years, we always had "tramps" or "hobos" who came to the door. My mother always fed them, but she had them stay out on the back steps. She always would fry them some potatoes, a couple eggs, and maybe give them some bread and butter and a little coffee. She always fed them, but she never let them in the house, even though it was much safer in those days.

And I always heard stories about how my father had saved the Reynolds State Bank. He went around and told all his friends and neighbors not to take their money out of the bank, but to leave it in the bank. It was one of the few banks that never closed. I don't know if the Reynolds State Bank still exists,[2] but my dad was the one who helped keep it open—rather like the old Jimmy Stewart movie. Dad was very social and very well-respected in the community. He was a pretty intelligent man. He had had two years of college at St. Ambrose College, in Davenport, Iowa.

Later, when my brother Tom was having financial problems, the bank was willing to loan him money to see him through.

A MAN WOULD COME TO TOWN WITH A MOVIE PROJECTOR, AND HE'D SHOW ONE OR TWO MOVIES IN A HOUSE THAT HE HAD RENTED.

- MILDRED HAYNIE -
(Born October 2, 1921)

My name is Mildred Haynie, and I am one hundred years old. I live in Cody, Wyoming. I live eleven miles out of town.

I was born on October 2, 1921, in my aunt's home in a little town in Colorado. Just now I can't remember the name of the town. My mother had gone down there to stay with her aunt until my arrival. But then we stayed there until I was two years old, because my mother was ill at the time. Then we came back to Wyoming and to the ranch where my folks lived. We lived out in the country, not too far from Pinedale, Wyoming.

Our ranch was a very small ranch, which my dad had gotten from other members of the family. They didn't do much with it, other than run wild horses on it to increase the herd. I don't recall exactly what they did because I was just a kid, and I wasn't at all interested in what they were doing.

Later, we lived in a very, very small town. Most of the people were ranchers, or in activities related to oil drilling. My parents and my older sister, Eileen, and I lived in a small house, and we were happy people. The house was nothing fancy, but it was adequate for us. There were two bedrooms, the living room, and the kitchen. My sister and I shared one of the bedrooms. It was very simple, but nice—adequate for us.

The house did not have indoor plumbing. We bathed in a metal tub. The house was heated by the wood stove in the kitchen and a coal stove. We had a well and a pump. We got our water from a pump which sat just outside the house, right on the porch, just outside the door. And we had a two-hole outhouse.

As you'd go out on the porch, you'd see an old swing set that my dad had put up for my sister and me, and a wood pile. Then beyond the little yard, there was a field, where the neighbors did some haying and kept some animals.

I first started grade school in a little one-room school. I went to that school just for first and second grade. After that, my grade school was in the high school. There were several classrooms, both upstairs and downstairs. The grade school was just a typical grade school. The teachers were pretty darn good. We had different teachers for the different classes. There weren't a lot of extracurricular activities, but we always had some type of music. Later, in high school, we had a marching band. I was in the band. I played the saxophone

As kids, we used to swim down in the creek. We also walked a lot. Sometimes we rode horses—when our friends had horses.

It was only in later years that we had movies. A man would come to town with a movie projector, and he'd show one or two movies in a house that he had rented. In those days, the movies were mostly about cowboys and Indians. I can't recall any specific movies that I saw. It wasn't a regular Saturday night routine. There would be movies just when he'd come through with the movies. Actually, there really wasn't very much going on in those days. The kids were all pretty good kids. You didn't hear about the kind of stuff that goes on today. We were kids that played out in the dirt and had fun.

From the time that we were first able to read, my mother saw to it that we had books of one kind or another. I still have some of the books she had gotten us. We really didn't have that many. We got others out of the school library.

There were people close by. I don't recall how many people lived in the little town where we lived, but there were people close by. The name of our town was Big Piney. We lived right in town, and walked to school every morning. We had to walk from one end of town to the other, but it wasn't very far. I'd walk home at noon for my lunch. In later years, when I was in high school, we'd go to other towns to play basketball and things like that.

My memory of the Depression era is not that sharp. It was a lot of years ago. I was just a teenager. I graduated from high school in 1939. As a kid, I really wasn't aware of the Depression. It just didn't mean too much to me. What I can remember is that the times were not too good for anybody.

As I said, my dad was a rancher. We didn't have a car, but Dad did have a truck. I was a teenager in high school when Dad got the truck. But I can recall that he'd go to the railroad in Campbell, Wyoming, and bring coal back to the people who lived around us. And he'd also bring back different things from the stores that they wanted or needed.

My mother was a good cook. She loved her plants. She'd plant flowers from seeds so she could have flowers in the summertime. She was an excellent horsewoman. She had a horse, and Dad would tell the local guys that they could ride her horse. But nobody could ride that horse, but Mom.

One thing that I can remember, is that men came to the vicinity where we lived via the railroad in Kemmer, Wyoming. They came to find jobs, food, and places to stay. Many found work, working for the ranchers. They stayed all summer to help put up the ranchers' hay.

CHAPTER 18

WE PLAYED BASEBALL IN THE ALLEY. IT WAS PRETTY HARD KEEPING THE BALL IN PLAY AND OUT OF THE NEIGHBORS' YARDS.

- CURT TREVOR -
(Born June 19, 1928)

I'm Curtis Trevor. I was born June 19, 1928. I would have been about one when "Black Friday" hit in 1929.

At that time, we lived on 16th Street in Moline, Illinois, near the old Trevor Hardware Store, which has since been torn down.

My dad was an attorney. My mother was a homemaker. There were six in our family. My mom and dad, two brothers, one sister, and myself. I was the third oldest child. I went to Willard School in Moline for grade school. I don't think it exists anymore.

During those years, there were out-of-work people called "hobos" who would come around and beg for food. My mother would feed them. They would sit out on the porch and eat. It was my impression that after Mom fed them, they would somehow "mark" our house to let others who might come along later know that the people in this house would give a them meal. I was so young that I don't recall whether they offered to work or not.

I can also remember men going up and down the alleys shouting, "Rags, old iron." Most often, they would just haul away whatever you gave them, but once in a while they might pay you something, if you gave them something worthwhile.

Most of my memories come from the years after we moved to 11th Avenue. That house was across the street from Allendale mansion. Allendale is now the administration building for the Moline public schools.

Our house there originally had an old, coal-burning furnace. We kids had to shovel coal into that old furnace. But then we got a stoker. The stoker somehow fed small pieces of coal into the furnace to keep the fire going. It moved coal into the furnace when the furnace needed more coal. It was kind of automatic. But you still had to take the clinkers—the cinders—out.

There was a window in the back of the house that was used to dump the coal into our basement. I think the coal men were able to back their truck all the way up to the window. They had a slide, which they would put in place. They were able to run their slide down from their truck through our basement window. The coal would then come roaring down the slide and fill up the coal bin.

My dad was an attorney. He got a job as an assistant attorney general down in Springfield, Illinois. Every Monday morning, he'd get up around 4 a.m. and drive down to Springfield. He'd stay through the week, and then would come home on the weekends. We were very fortunate that Dad was employed throughout the Depression. Our family had a steady income because my dad was working.

I only have vague memories of what we did for entertainment during those years. I can remember my folks taking us to a couple movies. They would have had to have been clean, funny movies. But I can't remember the names of them.

We listened to the radio. We always listened to *The Jack Benny Show* on Sunday night, if I remember correctly. Outside, we threw the baseball back and forth, and we even played baseball in the alley. It was pretty hard keeping the ball in play and out of the neighbors' yards. Sometimes it wasn't a hardball; sometimes it would be just a rubber ball.

Later on, we played a little tackle football. Looking back, that wasn't very smart. We didn't have the proper equipment. Somebody might have had a jersey. Somebody else might have had a helmet. Some of us had nothing. We could have gotten killed!

There was a vacant lot about a block away from us, and we played a lot of games on it. You could very easily hit a ball out of it for a home run. The ball would sail through the trees and fall into the street. Chasing it into the street was hard, not to mention dangerous. It was hard for the outfielders both to chase the ball down and then to get it back in.

Not far from that lot was a private residence with a swimming pool. Some of us would go up there and hope they'd invite us to go swimming. They never did. I don't blame them [laughing]. Then, of course, there was the Moline pool. It was about two miles east of our house. We'd walk down to it sometimes and go swimming. And there was the YMCA; that's where I learned to swim.

Mom sewed, cooked and cleaned, and did the "mom stuff." Some of my clothes were purchased at the store. J. C. Penney's was already around then, and we got a lot of stuff from Penney's. But I also got hand-me-downs. I had an older cousin. He'd outgrow stuff, and we'd get hand-me-downs from him.

CHAPTER 19

AT ONE TIME, THERE WERE THIRTY-SIX KIDS IN THAT SCHOOL, WITH ONE TEACHER AND EIGHT GRADES.

- NORMA LODGE -
(Born July 20, 1925)

I was born on July 20, 1925. I was born at home on our farm, in the farmhouse. In those days, the doctors made house calls.

My parents, my two sisters, and I lived on a farm in Atkinson Township, East of Geneseo, Illinois. One sister was older, and one was younger. My younger sister is still alive. She's in assisted living at Woodridge. My grandmother owned the farm, and my dad farmed it. That's where we lived, and that's where I grew up. I lived there until I got married.

The house was kind of a square house. The kitchen was sort of an add-on room, and there was a porch off of it. Off of the kitchen, there was the living room and the dining room. To the west, there was a bedroom, and to the north, there was another bedroom. So, there were five rooms downstairs, and there were four rooms, maybe five rooms, upstairs. None of the rooms had closets. The rooms in those days were built very simply. When I was younger, my bedroom was on the first floor; I later "graduated" to the second floor. I shared my bedroom.

Our farm was about 320 acres. All the farm that could be planted, was planted. Of course, there were farm buildings, and they sat on part of the total acreage.

We had animals: cows, horses, chickens, and pigs. Dad had horses for working the farm. We had a team of horses. In those days, you didn't have tractors. We had cows that were milked for income. We also had pigs that we sold to market. And we raised chickens for the eggs and the meat. So, we had meat, eggs, milk, and cream. I don't know how Dad kept the milk and cream.

On Saturday, we'd take the eggs and cream to town to the grocery store. They'd buy your eggs from you while you'd buy the groceries. Sometimes, you even took money home with you. We went to town in our car. Dad was a "Ford man." We never traveled by horse and buggy; that was before my time—during my mother's time.

My father raised corn. I don't recall if he also raised beans. In addition to the crops they raised on the farm, my mother and father also had a garden. My father worked very hard. Farmers didn't have the equipment then that they have now.

Of course, Dad did have some farm equipment. They didn't have combines in those days, but he did have or rent horse-drawn machines that would plow, plant, and pick the corn. The only time that I ever helped was when they rented a corn picker. We didn't own a corn picker, so we had to hire or rent one.

The first order of business was to "open" the fields of corn, by hand. You did that by handpicking the corn and throwing it into a wagon pulled by the horses. When we "opened" the fields, we would actually walk the fields, pick the corn, and throw it in the wagon. We had to do that before the corn picking machine went in, because it had to go where the corn was already picked. You had to have rows that had already been picked or cleared, otherwise the corn picker would run over the corn and ruin it. Today that's not necessary, but in those days the corn picking machine had to go outside the standing corn. So, we had to "open up" rows for it to go. The corn picker would be followed by a wagon, and the ears of corn would go into the wagon. The early corn pickers were similar to modern corn pickers, but they were not as well-made, mechanically. We handpicked to "open" the fields so we could use the machine.

We had a number of buildings on the farm. There was the house, a chicken house, and a barn where the cows were milked and where the horses were kept. There was also a holding park where the cows went at night in wintertime when it was cold. We also had a south barn where we stored hay. It was also a holding area for the cows.

In our house we had a furnace. But we didn't have electricity right away. We had kerosene lamps. Our kitchen was heated with the cook stove, which my mother had to start every morning. We normally burned coal, but you could burn wood if that's what you wanted to do or if you didn't have coal. She used corn cobs to start the fire, and then she put the coal or wood in after the fire got started. We had the corn cobs because you couldn't start the fire with just coal. It wouldn't catch. You needed something for a bed underneath. Then you'd put the coal on top of the bed of dried corn cobs, and then start the fire. Then the coal would catch fire.

We had a coal furnace in the basement. We later had a stoker, but not right away. The stoker came at a later time. You got the coal into the basement using a coal chute. You'd shovel the coal out of the truck onto the coal chute and it would slide down into the bin. And you also had a bin for corn cobs. That way, you'd have all the stuff you needed to start your fire: corn cobs in one bin and coal in another. The corn cob bin was not accessible by way of the window with the chute. The chute only went into the coal bin. I never had to start the fire in the furnace. I know my mother started fires in the cook stove in the kitchen. I didn't have much to do in terms of chores around the house; I just helped when asked.

The heat wasn't piped up to the second floor. There were, however, registers in the ceilings above the first floor. So, the upstairs was heated only by what went up through the registers and up the stairs. The stairway, of course, was open, so the heat would also go up the stairway.

We had no indoor plumbing. We of course had an outhouse. It was either a two-holer or a three-holer. In those days, we didn't have good toilet paper. That's what you used old catalogs for. We used Sears and

Montgomery Ward catalogs. When the new ones came, the old ones went out to the outhouse.

I can't recall the doctor coming to the farm, except when a baby was being born. You didn't call them for every little thing like you do now. You did your own doctoring.

When I started school, I went to Spring Creek School. It was a country school a-mile-and-a-half away. At one time, there were thirty-six kids in that school, with one teacher for all eight grades. We had a very strict teacher, but she was very good. She started teaching there when I was in first grade, and she retired when I was in eighth grade. Her name was Sarah Graham. As I said, she was a very strict teacher. If you dropped your pencil, you stayed in at recess time. She would take the grade she was teaching up on a platform. For example, if it was reading time for the second grade class, she'd have them go up on the platform and sit in little chairs, while the rest of us did our lessons that we had been assigned to do at that time. There were no out-of-school or extra-curricular activities in those days.

We went on to Geneseo High School, and out of that school there were two valedictorians and a salutatorian. I'm talking about the old Geneseo High School, which is gone now. It was across from the park, by the Congregational church.

In high school, I played in the band. I played the saxophone. The football team played at the old athletic field and the band played during halftime. Then, we had to walk back to the high school and change out of our uniforms. If we wanted to see the rest of the game, which was almost over by the time we changed out of our uniforms, we had to walk back out to the athletic field.

As kids we played baseball and tag. We had swings and teeter-totters. We had a radio. We listened to whatever was on the radio, but I can't recall the particular shows to which we listened. But that's what we did.

There was a movie theater in Geneseo, but we didn't go very often. I'm too old now to recall any specific movies that I might have seen.

My mother sewed our clothes. She both repaired our clothes and made new ones, as well. She made dresses, tops, pajamas, and stuff like that for us girls. She didn't make pants. We didn't have a lot of clothes, you know. Just what was necessary. And my mother darned socks. She repaired socks until they couldn't be repaired anymore.

In those days, I was just a kid. I was well fed. I didn't complain about anything.

CHAPTER 20

SOME AMERICANS . . . BELIEVED THAT THE CAPITALISTIC SYSTEM OF THE U.S. WAS FALTERING, AND THAT IT SHOULD BE ABANDONED AND REPLACED WITH THE RUSSIAN SYSTEM.

- FRANK LYONS -
(Born April 8, 1930)

My name is Frank Lyons, or to be more precise, Francis W. Lyons. My parents were William and Mary C. (Donohoe) Lyons. I was born on April 8, 1930, in Yankton, South Dakota. I was the second of seven children. I had five brothers and one sister. My youngest brother and my sister were twins. My mother was a very well-educated woman, and my dad was very supportive of her. My father was a farmer.

In those days, Yankton had a population of about nine thousand. It had formerly been the capital of the Dakota Territory, which had consisted of the Dakotas and parts of Montana and Wyoming. Yankton was an historic river town. For a while it was a very corrupt town. But money was made there, and quite a few substantial homes were built there. My Uncle Jack had a business in town that employed some seventy-five people. It made chicken crates, wooden egg crates, and pallets.

Our 120-acre farm was about three-and a-half miles from Yankton, and was situated near the confluence of the Missouri and James Rivers.

The land had been hacked from the willows and the cottonwoods along the Missouri River. The farm had the usual set of buildings, which included a barn, a hog house, and a machine shed. My parents bought the farm in 1929. That was not a good year to buy farms. By the end of the year, the stock market had crashed, and the "Great Depression" was upon us.

The Great Depression was the dominant event of the 1930s. It overwhelmingly influenced the lives of my parents, as it did most Americans. It is not easy for anybody born in the years after World War II, who has lived through an almost continuous seventy-five-year period of American wealth and prosperity, to understand the hardships that average Americans faced during the 1930s. It was not just a time of belt-tightening and waiting for good times to return. It was a time of hunger and privation. It was an era of bankruptcies and the loss of all assets that a family had accumulated. It was a time in history when many Americans lost confidence in their government and in America's free-enterprise system.

It was also an era of bank closings. Customers lost overnight every dime they had deposited in savings. The Federal Deposit Insurance Corporation (FDIC), which today insures bank deposits, was not yet in existence.

As if to make things worse, It was also an epoch of mortgage foreclosures. Farmers and homeowners had borrowed money from the banks to buy their farms and build their homes. Then the Depression hit. Suddenly those farmers and homeowners, who didn't have money to pay what they owed on their mortgages, watched helplessly as banks foreclosed those mortgages and took their farms and homes.

For many folks, the Depression was such a devastating psychological experience that they could not cope. It was not uncommon for men to abandon their families, commit suicide, or to go into deep psychological depression. The long duration of the Depression made it a way of life for a generation of people. Even after the Depression ended, some people were too scared to ever resume a normal life. Few of today's social "safety nets" for the needy existed in the early 1930s.

Some Americans thought that Russia, since its 1917 revolution and conversion to communism, was developing a workable, utopian plan to provide for their social, economic, and political security. They believed that the capitalistic system of the US was faltering, and that it should be abandoned and replaced with the Russian system. The horrors of the revolutionary Russian system were not yet known in the West. A benighted Lincoln Steffens, upon returning from a "sanitized and controlled" trip to Russia said, "I have been over in the future, and it works!"

But somehow, Dad and our family survived the Depression. We did not even lose our farm. Dad farmed with horses. He raised about 125 cattle, 125 hogs, and the same number of chickens. We survived by selling the cattle and hogs. He also raised corn, barley, and alfalfa.

Our farmhouse was spacious, but not at all grand. The prior owners had originally built a log cabin. That was long gone. Our house, after being built, was subsequently enlarged. It was built in three sections. It had eleven rooms. There were six rooms on the first floor: a kitchen, a dining room, a living room, a parlor, a room with a bathtub in it, and porch. There were front and back stairways to the upstairs. On the second floor, there were five bedrooms. There was a furnace in the basement. When money was tight, we burned wood; when times were good, we burned coal. The heat came up from the furnace through a four-foot-square register in the dining room floor.

Because the upstairs was unheated, we rarely went up there during the winter, except to go to bed. And during the South Dakota winters, the upstairs could get pretty darn cold. You'd get up in the mornings and there would be frost on the bedroom windows. I shared my bedroom and bed with my brother, Pat. The chimney from the furnace came up through our room, and sometimes for warmth, we'd hug the chimney.

When we lived there, it was a happy home for ten people. There were nine in my family, and we had a maid, Leona, who worked for us. She was paid $3.50 per month. Over time, she became part of the family. So, at dinnertime, there would be ten people around the table, and perhaps a hired man to boot. When we six boys were too young to help on the farm, my dad, from time to time, hired various men to help. It was a happy home. Mom and Leona shared the cooking and the canning. Our relatives still live in that old house, even now.

The house did not have electricity until 1941, when the efforts of the REA kicked in. Then we got 110-volt service. Except for the hand pump in the kitchen, there was no running water in the house. But the water table sat only about twenty feet below the house, and a pipe came up through the basement to the kitchen pump. Except for chamber pots, there were no indoor toilet facilities. We had a two-hole outhouse. The women used that. The men often relieved themselves elsewhere outside.

During the Depression years, there were, of course, some hand-me-downs, but I don't remember too many. What I can recall is receiving a big bale of World War I overcoats, pants, and shirts from Dad's uncle. We wore those things to school.

For grade school, I attended a one-room school, Willowdale District #3. It was about a three-minute walk from my home. There were two outhouses: one for girls and one for boys. And there was a barn on the property, where the kids who rode horses to school could leave their horses. But when I was there, only one boy rode his horse to school, and his family had made arrangements for him to leave his horse on our farm, where he could get food and water throughout the school day.

In Yankton, there was a big Benedictine community of perhaps five hundred Roman Catholic priests and nuns. They ran a number of grade schools, a high school, a college, and a hospital and medical center. When times got better, my parents sent my sister and my three younger brothers to the Benedictine schools. My sister later became a nun, and her twin brother, who had served Mass for the priests, became a priest. Eventually, they both left the religious life, and they each got married.

I was born in the Benedictine hospital. The Benedictines would hold ice cream socials, and they produced plays and musical events from time to time. My brother Jack developed musical and theatrical talents when he was very young. He would write plays, and he formed a seven-piece country band.

For entertainment, we played sports, especially kitten ball. It was played with a five-inch softball. And we played a lot of cards. We did not have a radio, because we did not have electricity. There were batteries in the basement, left by the previous owner for running a radio on 32-volt direct current. They didn't work very well. And we hunted. At first, I used a .22 caliber rifle, and later, 20- and 12-gauge shotguns.

I can recall that we had two cars, but no trucks. We had a 1928 Dodge, and later a 1936 Dodge.

What I can remember best about the '36 Dodge is that it had a railing across the backseat which was attached to the back of the front seat. You'd hang blankets over the railing to keep warm in the back seat because the car had no heater.

Early in the Depression, the federal government, led by Herbert Hoover, could not come to grips with the country's rapidly collapsing economic and social institutions. There was no model for the government to follow. The government was paralyzed. It seemed incapable of developing urgently needed plans and decisive action. The country was in despair. Instead of offering action and hope, the government recited platitudes such as, "Prosperity is just around the corner."

In 1933, Franklin Delano Roosevelt was inaugurated as president of the U.S. He immediately took vigorous, "tree shaking" action on all fronts to have the government radically rebuild the country's collapsing economic and social systems. He gave the country hope with his jaunty, confident presence in the White House. He understood how to use the radio to communicate with the American people with his periodic "fireside radio chats," broadcast from his family's ancestral home on the Hudson River. The measured tones of his cultivated and confident voice made most people feel that their government was now in good hands.

President Roosevelt traveled a road strewn with obstacles. The entrenched, "status quo" politicians did not easily give way to his recovery programs, which they saw as "socialistic" and radical, and as a betrayal of the established principles of self-reliance upon which the country was built. The new programs soon started to provide relief for the dire needs of the people, but the end of the Depression did not come until the early 1940s, with the advent of World War II.

In spite of the severe economic difficulties, as I said above, my parents managed to hang on to the ownership of their farm. Millions of farmers in the country were less fortunate. My dad's own parents lost their farm in 1937 because they could not pay their small bank loan of $1,600 to the Federal Land Bank. They had paid off the loan on their homestead earlier, but they then used it as collateral to buy additional land for a cattle pasture. But when they could not make the mortgage payment, they lost their home, farm, and the new pasture. They never recovered, and had to live the rest of their lives on the meager largess of their children.

Similar heartrending stories became the norm throughout the Midwest. My mother often said that because everyone else was in the same boat during the Depression of the 1930s, there was no feeling of personal inadequacy for being in such rocky economic straits.

There were but few opportunities for earning extra money to supplement the virtually nonexistent farm income. One, however, did arise for Dad, for a brief period of time. The county undertook a road improvement project to provide ditches and higher crowns for the rudimentary dirt roads near the farm. Dad worked on the road crew. He brought along a team of horses and a "fresnoe." A fresnoe was a dirt scraper with a flat cutting edge and a capacity to move about one cubic yard of earth. It skidded along the ground as the dirt was hauled to its destination. For a long day's work, he and the horses earned $5.00. At a time when people stood in line to find work for a dollar per day, this amount of money was like manna from heaven.

Uncle Bob Lyons, who was in his teens during the 1930s, signed up for the CCC (Civilian Conservation Corps), one of President Roosevelt's "alphabet soup" relief programs designed to invigorate the economy. He worked in the Black Hills of western South Dakota, building mountain roads, recreational areas, and resort hotels. For this he was paid

$21.00 per month. A portion of this meager wage was deducted from his pay by the paymaster and sent directly home to his parents. Some of the CCC participants started to receive "square meals" and to live in clean, orderly quarters for the first time in many years.

Although it was common for people to poke fun at the inefficiency, low quality, and poor management of the CCC, WPA (Works Progress Administration), and other "make work" government programs, the criticism was largely unwarranted. The programs provided positive results, injecting a trickle of cash, and perhaps a little hope, back into the paralyzed economy. Eighty-five-year-old sidewalks, roads, resorts, and structures, built by the WPA, still exist and show evidence of the high quality of the work. Work opportunities for intellectuals, writers, and artists were also provided. Libraries still stock their shelves with books by writers funded by the WPA. In South Dakota, the Yankton City Hall, including its murals, was a WPA project.

Some businesses failed during the Depression because it was no longer socially acceptable for affluent people, who were financially shielded from the Great Depression, to display their wealth. Those who could afford to buy costly, racy, custom-bodied Dusenbergs and stylish, three-ton V-12 Pierce-Arrows no longer did. Instead, they bought boxy Buicks and stodgy Chryslers. The luxury automobile industry in the US disappeared. Opulent living was prudently hidden behind closed doors. The excesses of the wealthy, as disclosed in F. Scott Fitzgerald's *The Great Gatsby*, were over. Wealth was not as much fun when it could not be publicly flouted!

During the Great Depression, life was especially hard on young people. Many were deprived of an education because of the lack of money. But for those with enough determination for self-improvement, a way was generally found.

My dad's nephew, James Lyons, arrived at our farmhouse door in the mid-1930s. He had driven twenty-five cattle 110 miles from his father's ranch in south-central South Dakota to market, and sold them there for a few dollars. Then, he worked until the farmer saw his crops "dried out" (burned out by drought). After that, he hitchhiked and walked another sixty miles to our place. James was a cheerful young man with an indomitable spirit. Dad and Uncle Francis Donohoe hired him as a farm hand for seventy-five cents per day. They put his wages in an education fund. At the end of the farm season, Mom and Uncle Francis took James to the nearby Southern Normal College in Springfield, South Dakota, and watched him as he placed his money on the registrar's table. James said, "I want to enroll, but this is all I have." The superintendent arranged a work-study program for him so he could start his college education. Although the Depression broke the spirit of some people, it toughened up James and many others, so that nothing in their lives would ever again seem insurmountable.

James's father, Uncle Dennis Lyons, was a pioneer settler on the remote South Dakota prairie. In 1910, at the age of twenty-one, Uncle Dennis had driven to Rosebud County with his new sixteen-year-old bride, the daughter of a blacksmith. They traveled in freight wagons full of goods. Uncle Dennis, his father, and my dad, who was no more than a boy, drove the three teams of horses. For $1,600 and a six dollar donation to an Indian welfare fund, Uncle Dennis bought a "relinquishment" and, with high hopes for a prosperous future, started his adult life as a rancher. A "relinquishment" resulted when the original homesteader abandoned the land.

A quarter century later, in 1933, Uncle Dennis, in the fashion of Irish writers, reflected on his life through his years in Rosebud County.

> [I live] with the dreams of 25 years vanished, with fancy's pictures faded, with youth gone, and age here. I live with economic disaster spreading despair in its wake—with drought and grasshoppers making the land uninhabitable. But from the human heart, springs hope eternal, and in the active hours of daylight with sober logic born of experience, I can see again a future. . . .

Even though the Great Depression hung over Bill and Mary, my mom and dad, like a pall, they shielded their children from most of its stresses and hardships. For their children, growing up on the farm during the Depression was a happy, easygoing experience. Life seemed normal.

CHAPTER 21

I REMEMBER COMING HOME FROM SCHOOL ONE DAY. MY DAD WAS UP ON THE ROOF OF THE BARN, PUTTING A POLE UP ON THE VERY PEAK OF THE BARN. THERE WAS A SECOND, SIMILAR POLE ATOP THE HOUSE, AND THERE WAS A WIRE BETWEEN THE TWO. THAT WAS THE AERIAL FOR THE RADIO.

- HELEN FAYE GREEN -
(Born January 10, 1917)

I was born on January 10, 1917. That makes me 103 years old . . . and a half. I was an only child. We lived on a farm so we had plenty to eat. We raised the food. We ate what we grew. We didn't buy very much, because we just didn't have much money.

The farm was six miles north of DeWitt, six miles from Welton, and six miles from Charlotte [laughing]. Today we're much closer to the Quad Cities.

Our farm was 160 acres. My dad bought the farm when the price of land was high. I was a kid, so I wasn't really aware of prices or anything. Prices then went down on all the commodities, livestock, and grain. Land prices went down, too, but he had already bought it at the high price, so he lost it. He lost it in the twenties before I was in my teens.

Probably when I was ten or eleven—maybe twelve. To tell the truth. I don't exactly remember. I think that the Depression hit the farmers before it hit the townspeople. Dad had paid a lot for the land, but then the prices of crops went down. His sister and brother-in-law had loaned him money to buy the farm, so they took the farm over. They had it for a while, and then they lost it, too. It was a very rough time. After my father had lost the farm, we rented it and continued to live there.

We raised cows, pigs, and chickens on the farm. And Dad had horses. He had six or more horses. He'd hitch them up to the wagon, the hay rack, the manure spreader, the planter, and the cultivator. The crop rows had to be quite a ways apart because there had to be enough room for a horse to go between the rows of corn. Sometimes, a corn stalk might be missing. Perhaps mice had eaten it. When that happened, my mother and I would put pumpkin seeds in the ground to fill in the missing spot. We had a lot of pumpkins. In the fall we'd gather them up and put them in the barn. We chopped them up and the cows and chickens ate them. And of course, we did too, in pies.

Besides corn, dad planted oats, as well as clover, alfalfa, and timothy. He always planted timothy because, at that time, it was thought that clover was too rich for the horses and that the horses had to have timothy grass. So, he grew some of both. After the oats were harvested, the next year he planted clover and timothy for fodder. Then, he'd go back to corn again. He had a rotation. He went from corn to oats to clover and timothy.

There, of course, were other buildings on the farm besides the barn. There was a corn crib, and there was a chicken house. Through the years, Dad replaced the chicken house and the corn crib and built new ones. There also was a hog house, which was a lean-to against the barn. And there was a machine shed, a granary, a garage, and a wash house. The wash house housed the washing machine. There was a little gasoline engine, which they would start up. It was attached to the washing machine with belts, which would run the washing machine. That's where they washed the clothing. Then the washed clothes were put through a ringer and rinsed in a tub, and finally they were hung out on the line to dry.

The house on the farm was fairly new. It had been built in the early twenties. We didn't build it. It was there when my dad bought the farm. Part of the old house was still there, too. It became a granary and Dad's workshop.

Our house was a typical square house. There were four rooms downstairs and four rooms upstairs. There was also an attic. Downstairs we had a living room, dining room, bedroom, and kitchen. There were four bedrooms on the second floor.

The house was heated with stoves. There was a cook stove in the kitchen. That's where, in the summer, we cooked the meals. We put corn cobs, wood, coal, or whatever we had in it for fuel. It was black, with lids instead of burners, which you would lift off with lifters.

Besides the stove in the kitchen, there was a little work table. Today, that little work table is out in my garage; I still have it!

There were also a table and chairs for eating. Directly over the table, a kerosene lamp had been hung from the ceiling. It was very nice, and gave us very good light.

We didn't have an icebox. There was a pantry that had shelves in it. That's where the dishes were kept. The flour and sugar were also kept there, in barrels. Cocoa, baking powder, and the like, were also kept in the pantry.

The dining room had a table and chairs around it. And that's actually where we lived. There was a stove in the dining room. When we had enough money, we used a hard coal stove which was wonderful. It was much like a stove that was made later, which was called a "Warm Morning" stove. When you'd get up in the morning, it would be warm. It was good, but it was a little more expensive. Probably, I suppose, because with the other types of stoves, we could burn cobs. We'd pick the cobs up after we'd feed the pigs the ears of corn. We'd go out with gloves on, after the pigs had eaten the corn off the cob, and we'd pick up the cobs. We'd let them dry out. Then we would burn them. There were always gloves in the basket for picking up those dirty cobs that we used in the stove. They burned well. I had even heard that some people burned corn cobs instead of coal for heat. I never saw that done. We didn't do it.

There was a creek running through our farm, with trees growing along it. Dad would let the trees grow until they were big enough to provide firewood. Then he would cut them down, saw them up, and burn them in the stove.

The living room was rather bare. It had a library table, a rocking chair or two, and several other chairs. And that was about it. It wasn't used much. There was no stove in the living room. Between the dining room and the living room, there was a sliding door that recessed back into the wall. In the summer that door was left open. There was also a front porch. Doors from both the living room and dining room opened onto the porch. In the summertime, those doors and the kitchen windows would be left open and the breeze would blow through. That was nice. The front porch wasn't screened in; it was just an open porch.

And there was a cellar underneath the kitchen. That was the place where we stored apples in the fall. We had shelves there. I think the apples were all Greenies. They weren't good when we picked them. We put them on a shelf in the cellar and it seemed like they ripened there through the winter. Later on, they were good to eat. We had other varieties of apples, too—Transparents and other kinds. And we had grapes and cherries.

There were no bathrooms in the house. We had an outhouse out back of the house. There were two seats and a lower seat for children; it was about half the height of the other seats.

We had a windmill and a supply tank. There was always wind, and the windmill would pump water into the supply tank. The supply tank was raised up a bit so that the water would flow from the supply tank through a pipe into the house. So, we had water in the house, but we didn't have a drain from the house. We had a pail under the faucet in the corner of the kitchen. When the pail would get full, we'd have to throw it out.

There was also a closed-in porch between the kitchen and the summer kitchen. The summer kitchen sat over the cistern. In the summer kitchen, there was a big sink and a hand pump that sat above the cistern. The water came straight up from the cistern through the hand pump. When it rained, we always let some of the water run away in the eaves. After it rained a bit, and after we thought the leaves had been washed out of the eaves, then we would divert the water into the cistern. Then we had soft water. About once a year, my dad would go down into the cistern and clean it out.

My mother raised chickens. In the spring, the hens would want to sit on eggs. They were called "cluck hens." She'd take them, and put them in a little building and give them a nestful of eggs to sit on. I think they'd sit on them for about three weeks, and then the little chickens would hatch. My mother had a little tent where she would feed the baby chicks. It was only two or three feet tall. The little chickens could get in there and eat, but the hens couldn't, so the little chickens were able to get something to eat. She raised a lot of chickens, so she had eggs to sell. We sold eggs to a hatchery. That would be in the spring.

Mom had a big garden. She raised carrots that she picked and put in a crock with sand over them to keep them. She raised parsnips, but left them in the ground until spring, and then she would dig them up. They were so much better in the spring. They were so much sweeter when they were left in the ground over the winter.

Mother helped to milk the cows. She cleaned the separator.

She did the laundry, the ironing, and the mending. There was a lot of mending in those days because the clothes were made out of cotton. It seemed to me that the men would wear their socks only once, and they'd already have a hole. She did a lot of darning of socks.

We ate what we raised. We had chickens, cows, and pigs. Sometimes we ground corn in a coffee grinder and made corn meal for corn bread.

Sometimes we had a radio, and we'd listen to the radio if we had a battery for it. Our radio was maybe a six-inch cube, but it was a good radio—when we had a battery for it. The battery looked rather like a modern car battery.

I remember coming home from rural school one day. My dad was up on the roof of the barn, putting a pole up on the very peak of the barn. There was a second, similar pole atop the house, and there was a wire between them. That was the aerial for the radio.

We thought we were in heaven! We could listen to Nashville, Tennessee. My mother liked to listen to Nashville. As a child, I can recall listening to WBBM in Chicago. They had a program for children. Exactly what shows I listened to, I just can't remember.

We had to walk a half mile to get the mail. Sometimes I'd get it, and sometimes the neighbors did. We'd get our mail and also the neighbors' mail, and they did the same.

I went to a rural school for grade school for eight years. Then I went to high school in DeWitt. The rural school was three quarters of a mile from our house. I walked to it. It was great.

When I was little, there were some bigger boys, in seventh or eighth grade, and they would fill the blackboard up with numbers. I thought that was wonderful. I'd go home and fill my little blackboard up with meaningless numbers. When I got to multiplication and division, I was so glad, because I finally learned to fill my blackboard up with meaningful numbers.

The rural school had one room with a potbelly stove in the middle. In the morning we'd all sit around the stove, boys on one side and girls on the other. We'd get chilblains on our feet from the cold as we walked to school. Chilblains were frosted feet that would itch as they got warm. The floor in the schoolroom was cold. There was nothing under the floor. I can recall my dad taking newspapers and wrapping them around my feet before my feet went into the five-buckle overshoes. Back then, the snow wasn't even taken off the road. We had to walk through it. But if the drifts got very high, then my dad would take me on horseback to get through the snow drifts.

The school had no indoor facilities. For water, we had to climb over a fence, walk across a farm field, and then climb over another fence to get to a neighbor's windmill to get water. Then, when we came back, we had to reverse the process. That's the way we got water for the school.

The field that we crossed was always a pasture. There was never corn in it. It was always something we could walk across. The farmer never had livestock in it while we were in school. It was fenced, but he had a stationary gate for us that was down low so we could easily crawl over it. The farmer and his wife had no children, and I think they just kind of took care of us. They had water at their place for us, and they had this "gate," so we could easily climb over it. There was no corn growing there for us to get lost in.

And I remember when we each had to bring our own cups. Before that, we all had to drink out of one dipper. And I remember when we had to bring our towels to school to wash and dry our hands. I think we all washed in the same water. There'd be a puddle of water outside where we threw it out after we had washed our hands.

I had one teacher for first grade, and then I had another teacher for the next two or three years, and then one for the last four years, who was an aunt to everybody but me. They called her by her first name, Bernadine, and I called her Bernadine, too. But there was no disrespect in that.

The number of kids in this one-room school varied. I think some days, I was the only one there. Some of them, to get to school, had to go across fields, and some of them had to walk maybe from a mile beyond our place. When the weather was bad, they didn't make it. On a nice day, maybe a half dozen kids would be in school.

All the grades were in the same room, and we learned from listening to the others. That's why I was so anxious to find out what all those numbers on the board meant. Kids in separate grades, like they are now, wouldn't have the anticipation that we had.

In those days, you'd hear what was being taught, over and over. If you forgot it, you'd hear it again in the next grade.

For toilet facilities, there were two outdoor buildings. One for boys and one for girls. They were at each corner of the lot.

For lighting in the school, we had the sun and doors and windows. There were kerosene lamps, but they were only used if we put on a play or if there was a box social to raise money for something. The ladies would decorate a shoe box and put food in it, and then the men would bid on the box. The woman who made the box would eat with the man who made the highest bid. That's the way we raised money to get the blackboards. I heard them talk about it. We had straight blackboards.

My dad had a car. In the wintertime, it was put up on blocks so that the weight wouldn't always be on the tires. It was a 1913 Ford Model T, I believe. We couldn't use it during the winter because the roads weren't plowed, so we'd put it up on blocks.

In the wintertime, I was either at home or at school. One time, there was a lot of snow, and people were getting short of supplies. So, all along the road to DeWitt, people got out with scoop shovels and shoveled a path for the cars to go through. A scoop shovel was a shovel they shoveled grain with. It was maybe eighteen inches to two feet across. Men were out shoveling all along the six miles to town. One car went in from each place or area, got supplies, and brought them back. Then the wind blew and blew, and the road was all shut down again. It blew in again that night, and we were snowbound again!

While we lived on the farm, salesmen would come by. There was the Bakers' man, the Watkins' man, and the McNess' man. They came and they sold spices, and I believe some other things as well. I don't recall exactly what all they did sell. I know they sold spices. They sold cinnamon, nutmeg, cloves, and vanilla. There were no stores nearby. They were six miles away.

For entertainment, we played a lot of cards. A lot of rummy and solitaire. We really didn't attend any church.

CHAPTER 22

WE BELONGED TO THE METHODIST CHURCH AND THEY HAD A WOMAN'S ORGANIZATION THAT WAS CALLED THE "GLEANERS." . . . [THEY] WOULD HAVE CLOTHES-PATCHING CONTESTS. . . . EVERYBODY WORE CLOTHES WITH VISIBLE PATCHES. . . . THEY HAD CONTESTS FOR WHO COULD MAKE THE NEATEST—THE BEST-LOOKING—PATCH.

- ROBERT SCOTT -
(Born September 16, 1923)

I was born on September 16, 1923. I had two brothers; no sister. My brothers were older than I was. We lived in Erie, Illinois. I was raised in the small town of Erie. We did not live on a farm.

Our home had electricity, and we had running water and inside facilities, which a lot of people then didn't have. My mother had a washing machine that had an agitator in it that went back and forth and washed the clothes, and it had a wringer.

I was about six years old when the Depression hit. My dad was a lawyer. He was a former president of the Rock Island County Bar Association. I would say that his practice went reasonably well during the Depression. Of course, we were in a farming area, and many of his clients were farmers. When they came to pay their bills, they would sometimes bring in livestock—mostly chickens. They would put them in a gunny sack and bring them in. And he'd give them credit for each chicken. I don't remember how much a chicken was worth. It wasn't very much. Then, he'd bring them home, and we three boys would open up the gunny sack and take out the chickens. We'd put their heads down on a block of wood, with the head extending over a bit. We had a hatchet, and then with one fell swoop, we'd chop off the head of the chicken, and then throw the chicken out in the yard, and watch it run around—with its head chopped off. They would actually run around and fly with their heads off. Then all of a sudden, they would conk out, and that would be it. It was amazing how far they would go . . .

My mother didn't work outside the home after my parents were married. It wasn't the thing for women to work in those days. The government and society frowned on a family that had two wage earners in the same family. At that time, there were too many families that didn't have any wage earner at all. To have two wage earners—both the mother and father working—was a "no-no" back in those days. My mother, before she married, worked at a department store in Erie—if you can believe that! In those days, Erie was kind of a going town. Before the Depression hit, it also had a bank, a couple grocery stores, and a hardware store.

The biggest memories I have of the Depression were of the prices. Gasoline sold at eighteen cents a gallon, and that was pretty much all taxes. Eighteen cents! And of course, in those days, you'd go to a gas station, and the attendant would come out and wash your windshield and put the gas in the car.

Another thing that I remember is that there really wasn't any class distinction in Erie. There was no upper class, no lower class, and no middle class. There were just no classes. Nor were there any colored people in Erie. I had never had any personal contact with a colored person until I went to Augustana College in Rock Island, Illinois. I didn't understand what all the fuss was about.

We belonged to the Methodist church, and they had a woman's organization that was known as the "Gleaners." My mother belonged to that organization. The "Gleaners" would have clothes-patching contests. Back in those days, women did a lot of patching. Everybody wore clothes with visible patches. If you wore blue jeans, you'd have a patch. You'd have patches all over. And they had contests to see who could make the neatest—the best-looking—patch. And they'd patch the hole from both the outside and the inside of the hole.

Nevertheless, most of our clothes were purchased at the store. My mother did make some clothes for herself, and occasionally for us. But for us, most of our clothes were bought at the store. But then, I was the youngest of three boys, so, you know where I fit in on the clothes chain. I got all the hand-me-downs. They weren't hand-me-downs from another family or anything like that; I got them from my brothers. One was six years older, and the other was two years older. The one who was two years older was growing fast. He'd get new clothes, and I'd get his hand-me-downs. Of course, my mother and the other women all darned socks.

I went to both grade school and high school in Erie. The school was right in the middle of the village, and it had three stories. Each teacher taught about thirty kids. There was one teacher and no helper. There were two grades to a room. In one room, you had first and second grade. The third and fourth grades were in another room. The kids were very respectful of the teachers. There wasn't as much horsing around. Of course, kids will always be kids. But what I am saying, is that the kids were well-behaved, as I remember.

As I said, there were about thirty kids in each room. A bell would ring, and we would go to different rooms for different classes. I can remember going to the music room. And we had a manual arts room for the boys, where we learned to use a saw, hammer, and things of that sort.

My parents had a garden. We all tended it all summer long. It was a good garden. We raised little onions, tomatoes, and potatoes. And we also raised them in grandmother's yard. She, too, had her home in Erie. She had a big garden. Mom and all the women canned. They would always be proud of how many quarts of "this and that" they canned. Actually, they used glass quart Mason jars, with the lids on top.

For entertainment, we had a radio—an Atwater Kent. That was the name of the radio. It had a big cabinet. It was a nice-looking piece of furniture. We had it for a long time before my mother died. We listened to *The Orphan Annie Show*. My favorite program was *The Jack Benny Show*. We used to listen to him on late Sunday afternoons. We'd turn on the radio, and everybody would sit down, or lay down on the davenport. Jack Benny was funny, and the language was great. There was no bad language or anything like that. He showed how it was possible to tell jokes and be funny without bad language. I thought his show was the best of all.

When something went wrong with the radio, or when you had to replace a tube, they'd turn the radio around with its face toward the wall to get inside of the radio. There really wasn't very much to it. The works were probably about a foot long and eight inches high. That was about it. We also had a theater in town. Most of the time it was open. I went to the movies quite a bit. I remember childhood movies. I remember mainly westerns. And I can remember *Gone with the Wind*, but that was later.

CHAPTER 23

YEARS LATER, MY MOTHER WORKED AT ST. JOSEPH'S ORPHANAGE. . . . AFTER CARING FOR HER OWN TWELVE CHILDREN, MY MOTHER CARED FOR THE YOUNGER CHILDREN THERE.

- S. M. F., OSF -
(Born September 27, 1926)

My name is S. M. F. I am using my initials because I am a member of a religious order. I was born on September 27, 1926. Doctor Dokery delivered me at our home. He was the same doctor who delivered all twelve children in my family. There were seven boys and five girls.

We lived in Oak Creek, Wisconsin. Oak Creek is situated directly south of Milwaukee. We lived at the north end of the Town of Oak Creek on College Avenue, across the street from the city of Milwaukee. I lived with my parents and siblings for fifteen years. The North Shore train line was ten minutes from our home. Of course, we were not allowed to walk the tracks.

My father had been a farmer in his younger days. When he asked my mother to marry him, she said that she would not marry if he remained on the farm. My father then took a job with the township of Oak Creek, where he worked for forty-two years. He did roadwork. Over the years, the township of Oak Creek expanded until it became the city of Oak Creek in 1950.

In May of 1935, the township established a volunteer fire department. Dad was one of the department's first twenty-nine members. The department at first had only one fire station and one fire truck—a 1935 Pirsch.

My mother had studied nursing, but she could not practice once she decided to marry. Nurses were not allowed to be married at that time. She therefore was a homemaker, until her twelve children grew older and began attending school. She then obtained employment at the airport, where she prepared trays of food for passengers on the planes. The trays were put together across the street, and then shipped over to the airport.

Years later, she worked at St. Joseph's Orphanage. Once St. Gerard's Church and School, with the passage of time it became a home for orphans. It was located on the south side of Milwaukee, at 18th Street and Oklahoma Avenue. The orphanage was operated by the Felician Sisters. It served boys and girls between the ages of three and sixteen. After caring for her own twelve children, my mother cared for the younger children there. I remember that my mother was always home from her job in time to greet us as we came home from school. St. Joseph's Orphanage is no longer there. It has since been replaced by St. Francis Hospital.

Our home was heated by a coal stoker, which was downstairs in our basement. I recall my father and older brother stoking the coals. The coal was stored on one side of the house. As the truck arrived to dump new coal for the stoker, the dust would make its way to the portion of the basement where my mother would do the laundry. Therefore, my father built a temporary wall to prevent this.

We had an electric stove in the 1920s, which my mother bought from the Spiegel catalog. I recall that my mother told us not to tell any of our friends about the electric stove—that would be "bragging!" But I think that she really feared that all of the neighbors would find out and ask to bring over their baking and turkeys to prepare in our oven.

We also had a telephone. Because my father was a volunteer fire-fighter, we were required to have one. His fire coat was always hung on the first hook, on the steps to the attic. His boots were also kept nearby, and they could not be moved. When the telephone rang to warn of a fire, our job was to grab my father's coat and boots and get them to him as quickly as possible.

At a later date, the town of Oak Creek installed an intercom in our house. My father instructed us that we should "never touch the button until I am home." He did not want us to be listening in on all of the township's emergency calls. The township only called when Dad was home.

There were two large rooms in the downstairs of our house. There was one large room upstairs. We slept two in a bed, and as a child, it somehow seemed that we always had plenty of room. I recall that dormers were later added—built onto the house. Anything to make more room for a new family member!

We had two iceboxes. I would wait for the iceman to come. There was a card that we set out to let him know how many pounds of ice our family needed. The iceman, who seemed to be the age of a college student, would arrive and put a chunk of ice on his shoulder. He would then carry and place the chunk of ice on the top shelf of the icebox. The water from the melted ice would drain to the bottom of the icebox.

My father and uncles also installed the indoor plumbing. We had a toilet in the 1920s. If it did not flush as it should, we would pour a pail of water in it.

We always had enough food. We had a large garden for vegetables alongside our house. My mother would can and make jelly. Our house stood on an acre of land. When my parents married, that acre of land had been given to them as a wedding gift. My grandma owned a plot of land from College Avenue to 6th Street. As her children grew and married, she would either give them either an acre of land, or five hundred dollars if they wished to live somewhere else. My parents sold a fifth of their acre of land to a neighbor. They needed the money, and the neighbor needed the land, so it worked out well.

We had a Model T Ford. To start it, my parents needed to crank the motor. My father needed a car all day, but I can remember my mother cranking up the car and driving it. My father did all of the grocery shopping. He often went to a grocery store at Tippecanoe, an early shopping district, which was on the corner of Howard and Howell Avenues. My mother kept ample supplies of oranges and bananas in our house. We ate a banana every day. Sometimes the grocer would give my father several extra oranges for our large family. A strip of stores, including an A&P, a National Tea, and drug stores lined the area. My brothers were hired at the drug stores.

My mother made all of our clothes. She was very particular about how her children looked when we went to school. I remember having to wear thick cotton stockings that extended over the knees until I was in sixth or seventh grade. My mother was always worried about her children being cold.

She even made us coats, using old drapes or thick material that she bought from the Goodwill store. My mother used an old Singer sewing machine to make our clothes. I did not own a coat that had been bought from the store until I entered the convent in 1941. We did have a family friend who would occasionally give us a coat for one of the children in our large family.

I recall that we had an old wringer washer that my mother used for laundry. She would never let us go near the washer, as she feared we would lose a limb in the wringer.

I have fond memories of attending St. Stephen's School. There was no kindergarten at the time that I entered first grade. Grades one through three were housed in old wooden barracks. They had been built during WWI to house the German prisoners of war. When the barracks were no longer needed after the war, they were used for our school.

After the war, some of the prisoners who had been housed in the barracks stayed in this country. The farmers hired them. I remember my mother telling us of young girls who would throw slips of papers with their addresses to prisoners in the barracks. She was very distressed to think of what a dangerous practice this could be.

I remember walking to school past the airport. I enjoyed school. We sat at long desks with two students at each one. They were sturdy desks, with heavy iron frames at the bottom. I had good experiences at St. Stephen's. Sister Susan was my teacher in the primary grades. We had our multiplication tables memorized! But we lacked books in our school. We used old library books that had been donated. I used to enjoy reading the *Father Finn* books. They were books about children in an orphanage. I read all of them. We all had Tippecanoe library cards and could take the books home to read.

I remember our required textbook, from the *Dick and Jane* series. "Dick ran. Jane ran." It seemed everyone in their family was always running. My father would sit in his big chair and smoke his pipe. Sometimes he would be reading the *Milwaukee Sentinel*, which came every morning. I was in first grade, and I would ask him to listen to me practice reading from my *Dick and Jane* book. My father would have me sit on the floor and he would listen to me while I read about Dick and Jane running. One day my father asked, "Is that all that's in that book?" I answered, "That's all for now."

We had a radio on most of the time in our house. It sat on a table. My mother loved taking us to the movies. I saw every Shirley Temple movie shown at the theatre on Mitchell Street. My brothers also had to attend Shirley's movies, whether they liked them or not! None of us could stay home alone. I do remember going to see *Steamboat Around the Bend* with my mother. She really admired Spencer Tracy; we all had to attend his movies with her. My father did not go with us to the movies.

The boys in my family played baseball in the backyard. They were very competitive. They also played some sort of football. I played with dolls. My mother bought a tall doll for my sisters and me. It actually said, "Hello." She sewed clothes for the doll. One day my brother broke open the back of the talking doll. He was curious about how it was able to say, "Hello!" He discovered a tape inside its back. My brother was in real trouble!

My father also enjoyed baseball. He would mow our lawn while ball-games were being broadcast on the radio. He would open the kitchen window and turn the radio on full blast so that he could hear the ball game while he was mowing the lawn.

I feel that FDR was the best president that we ever had because he encouraged people to work. He was an excellent speaker, and we often listened to his speeches on the radio. I remember the CCC planting trees everywhere. I also recall parks being built by the WPA.

I found my vocation during the Depression. My father and I both looked forward to attending Mass. The priests from the Redemptorist Retreat Center, in Oconomowoc, would lead the Mother of Perpetual Help devotions that we also attended each Tuesday evening. My parents could never attend Mass together, because someone needed to be home with the other children.

My primary teacher, Sister Susan, and two other sisters at St. Stephen's School inspired my vocation. Those sisters were so lovable and full of life. I can recall, when I was in seventh or eighth grade, how I enjoyed watching the sisters ride bicycles while wearing their full habits. They seemed so joyful.

Molthen-Bell Funeral Home was where family funerals were held. The doctors made house calls to deliver babies. The town of Lake had a school doctor and a school nurse. They would travel to schools within that area. The school nurse wore a navy blue uniform, which made her look very professional. When we returned to school after a long summer, she would check all of our heads of hair for head lice. She would ask the teachers if they suspected that any of their students had communicable diseases. If a student came down with symptoms of measles or mumps, the school nurse would take them home. She would give the family a large card that read "Communicable Disease." The family would then post that card in the window of their home. If someone in the house was diagnosed with a more serious illness, such as polio, a large black ribbon was tied to the door of the house.

A truck would deliver milk to our house on a daily basis. There were two dairies that delivered milk. Every day one of us had to take turns flagging down the milk truck. Sometimes we would run out of bakery goods. So, we also needed to take turns flagging down the trucks from the Jaeger or Omar bakeries. I found it very embarrassing to have to flag down the driver.

CHAPTER 24

THE GREAT THING ABOUT THE DEPRESSION YEARS WAS IT PAVED THE WAY FOR THE U.SA. TO EMERGE AS THE WORLD'S LEADER—AS THE PREEMINENT LAND OF OPPORTUNITY—THE LAND OF DEMOCRACY, INDIVIDUAL LIBERTIES, AND RELIGIOUS FREEDOM.

- ALBERT J. SAIA -
(Born November 19, 1933)

I was born in 1933. My family struggled during the Depression years.

My grandparents had all migrated here from Sicily. In Sicily, they were farmers or miners. They made sure their children learned English and got an education.

At an early age, we learned to go out and earn whatever we could to help our families. There were no allowances from Mom or Dad. Instead, we worked.

At twelve, I caddied and set pins at the local bowling alley. That's when I acquired my Social Security card and started paying taxes to Uncle Sam.

We wore hand-me-down clothes; our toys and bikes were also hand-me-downs or second-hand.

My closest friends grew up in the same environment. Several of us worked our way through college. We were all disciplined. We were part of what has come to be known as the "Greatest Generation." We lived through three wars—WWII, Korea, and Nam. We saw a lot of family members and friends go off to war. Some never came back.

The Depression years were tough, but America's character stood tall. When WWII came about, it brought us out of the Depression. America emerged, by war's end, as a worldwide industrial and manu-facturing power.

The great thing about the Depression years was it paved the way for the U.S.A to emerge as the world's leader—as the preeminent land of opportunity—the land of democracy, individual liberties, and religious freedom.

Chapter Notes

The chapter notes in this book are not essential to understanding any of the stories told in this book. They are included because they were important to the storytellers, and because I thought you might enjoy seeing some of the people, places, and things mentioned in these memoirs. I hope you do.

WILLIE MCADAMS—CHAPTER 1

The Tabernacle Baptist Church of Moline, IL, as noted by Willie McAdams, came into existence in 1904, when a small group of Moline settlers began meeting for worship services in each other's homes.

The church was officially organized in 1906. The church's members then bought a small lot at the corner of 8th Street and 16th Avenue around 1913, but later sold the property. They then bought a lot at the corner of 15th Street and 26th Avenue, and moved their church (the small white building below) there. In 1967, the original church was torn down and replaced with the church that exists today.

The Rev. R. A. Allen (above) pastored the Tabernacle Baptist Church for a half century—from 1936 to 1986. Rev. Allen baptized Willie, and was nearly rebaptized himself in the process. Pastor Allen pastored his congregation for thirty-one years in the little old church, and nineteen in the new.

SISTER FELICIA SCHLECHTER, OSF—CHAPTER 4

Sister Felicia's story is one of four stories given to me by Roman Catholic nuns. Each, while sharing their stories with me and allowing me to use their stories, specified how they wished their names to appear in my book. Sister Felicia allowed me to use her full name. R. T. S. (reserved for my next book) asked that only her initials be used. Sister Mariella (reserved for my next book) allowed me to use that much of her name. S. M. F. (Ch. 23) allowed identification only by her initials.

KAY CONWAY CORRIGAN—CHAPTER 16

1. Delco began providing lighting by use of a generator and batteries as early as 1918, as shown in this video: https://www.youtube.com/watch?v=Ho_ZDrVlDZw.

2. The Reynolds State Bank was founded in 1888 and remained in existence until February 27, 2021, when it merged with the Peoples' National Bank of Kewanee.

The cover of this book was created from a photo taken by the author on May 14, 2022, of St. Joseph's Cemetery in rural Mercer County, Illinois. In her story, Mrs. Corrigan tells how that cemetery came to be.

About the Author

John Donald O'Shea is a retired circuit court judge. During his twenty-six years on the bench, he handled the full gambit of cases, from major civil suits for money damages to, and including, divorces, adoptions, juvenile cases, non-support matters, eminent domain cases, suits for injunctive relief, and minor and major criminal cases, including three cases where the death penalty was sought. He spent most of the last ten years of his judgeship as Presiding Judge of the Criminal Division of the Circuit Court of Rock Island County, Illinois.

Prior to his 1974 election to the bench, he served as an assistant state's attorney, as Moline Corporation counsel, and as an attorney in private practice.

Don graduated from the University of Notre Dame (BA '64) and Notre Dame Law School (JD '65). Thereafter, he did his basic and advanced training with the Illinois National Guard before applying for a commission in the US Naval Reserve. He was commissioned therein as a lieutenant junior grade (JAG), and retired at the rank of lieutenant commander.

Don has previously published two books.

The first, *Memories of the Great Depression—A Time Forgotten*, was published and released by Crosslink Publishing on October 5, 2021. It is a compilation of the memoirs of thirty ordinary Americans who lived through the Great Depression of the 1930s.

The second, *The Stuffed Animal*, was published and released by Beacon Publishing on November 12, 2021. It is an illustrated children's Christmas story.

Don's author website can be viewed at https://johndonaldosheaauthor.weebly.com.

Since his retirement from the bench in 2000, Don has remained active. Besides playing golf and walking the course five days a week, Don has been a paid political op-ed writer for the *Moline Dispatch* and the *Rock Island Argus*, and more recently for the *Quad City Times*.

Don is also a published playwright. He has published eighteen plays with four different publishers. His first play, *Little Nell and the Mortgage Foreclosure*, published by Theatrefolk, has been his most popular. Two others, *The Day Ma's Boys Done Went to Town to Rob the Bank, Again*, and *The Day Black Bart Balderdash and Dangerous Dan McGrew Nearly Went to Dueling at Miss Kitty's Golden Nugget Saloon*, published by Big Dog Publishing, are among his personal favorites. His published plays can be viewed at his website for plays, http://www.osheasplays.com.

In his retirement, Don has also served as a volunteer theatrical director for two high schools and three junior highs. Don's daughter, Erin, a professional actress, has created the audiobook versions of Don's two books, and has served as his very valuable proofreader and "revision suggester."

Printed in the United States
by Baker & Taylor Publisher Services